CHORAL MUSIC
AND ITS PRACTICE

CHORAL MUSIC
AND ITS PRACTICE

by

NOBLE CAIN

M. WITMARK & SONS
Educational Publications
New York   N. Y.

FOREWORD

A foreword prefacing as such, things to come, may be a para-
doxical term when one begins such a foreword with a look backward. Yet in the history of the development of choral music in
America, a look backward reveals much that bears on things to
come. Certainly much that appears in the following pages is
the result of attitudes, aims, techniques and accomplishments
which have taken place far and wide in the field of choral activity, largely since the advent of the decade known as the
"twenties".

America, prior to that time, largely occupied with matters
pertaining to growth as a material nation, found itself at the
culmination of a definite period with the first world war. It
was as if the roughnesses and uncertainties of adolescent na-
tional growth had been smoothed out in the maturity of participation, as an equal member, in the scheme of world collaboration with countries much older than itself. Those things
of the old world which had been largely lost again became
prominent. Especially was this true in choral music, for, as
in separation from the mother country and the subsequent
growth of the pioneer expansion in church and state, choral
music adapted itself to the demands of the times. And these demands were not of liturgical or classical proportions. Rather
they were for matters of purely sense entertainment as distinguished from art perception and analysis. Thus the music

hall ballads, the cow boy songs, the negro minstrel shows, the
school glee clubs, the church choirs, found themselves furnishing music to suit the occasion, and the occasion was usually
recreation solely as recreation.

In the course of time with centralization in larger and
larger cities, there grew up a cultural life dependent, so far
as music was concerned, on the employment of the symphony
orchestra and the oratorio society for the reviving and bringing again to Americans the best products of the old world. For
here indeed in America, we had not yet grown old enough to
have evolved an art of our own. We had been too busy with the
plain facts of living. Outside of a few good symphony orchestras and a very few good oratorio societies, instrumental
and choral music was left to itself in most parts of the country.
To say that the music of the masters was given the greatest
consideration in programs of schools, churches, and independent societies would be stretching the point considerably.
As a matter of fact, many school, church and independent
musical society people were even ignorant that any such masters
existed, except in tradition or in catalogs of publishing houses.
And so up to the "twenties," the music of the general public,
even in the schools, consisted of light orchestra music and
glee club material, with here and there an operetta or a minstrel
show.

At the close of the first world war, the *a cappella* movement gained great headway and set the pace for all followers
of choral music, both in and out of the schools. With this
newly found style thrilling them, choral directors everywhere
began to organize and train choirs. A search was on for material. A renaissance of the art of good singing in groups took
the place of the soloist recital era. As in all recrudescences
of art, those in places of leadership began to look into the
sources of material. They eventually found themselves back

in the wealth of material furnished by the great men of all
time, Palestrina, Gabrieli, Vittoria, Byrd, Peter Phillips, Morley, Dowland and all the rest of the sixteenth and seventeenth
century pioneers and masters up to and including J. S. Bach.
The art of singing unaccompanied revived and gained again
some of the vitality which was lost when that band of pilgrims
and dissenters left forever the continent of Europe and all of
its cultural centers. America was on its way to a new era in
choral singing.

This opened up the field, especially in the public schools
and followed closely by the church, to a great and exhaustive
study of how to perform such music as it should be performed.
Problems of literature once settled, matters of style and of
interpretation became paramount issues involving the tone
quality of an ensemble, pitch fidelity, and many other questions eliciting a variety of solutions. It came to be recognized
finally, that basic procedure with the development of tone
quality was the development of the individual voice away from
fads and fanciful "effects" and toward a definite vocal building
as laid down by the masters themselves. The school of "effects"
was given impetus by the radio and theatre school and, as such,
branched off from legitimate choral singing. Good choral treatment still maintained certain standards of singing the vowels,
placing the voice so as to secure the most resonance combined
with color. A study of plain chant afforded much aid in the
matter of proper inflection. A definite school of legitimate
choral singing, devoid of effects, was established and began to
show amazing results. There are now practically thousands of
a cappella choirs scattered throughout a land which at the turn
of the century boasted but a few. These choirs today both in
school and in church are performing the music of the masters as
well as that of the moderns in the best prescribed manner.

"Choral Music and its Practice" attempts to comment on

some of the procedures which have made this great activity and knowledge possible to even the humblest school child. For a nation singing would not be complete without the singing of good music as well as unworthy music. And what is good music? Good music may be said to be that which takes the most time and labor in the learning, and which lasts the longest in the appreciative processes of the human mind, when once learned and made a part of the being. And America is now on the road to that sort of musical appreciation. Its succeeding generations of children are becoming more and more choral-conscious. It bodes well for the future both musically and culturally. Let those who have a part in this look well to it that they steer a straight course, adhering to the tried and true and not being swayed or turned aside by the seeming foibles of the moment.

CONTENTS

ix

CONTENTS

CHORAL MUSIC
AND ITS PRACTICE

CHAPTER I

THE AESTHETICS OF CHORAL MUSIC

Primitive man

Ever since the advent of Man as an articulate creature the possibility has existed that Man could sing. However primitive he may have been before he began to express himself in sounds from his throat and "voice-box," the fact remains that there arrived a time somewhere in his early history when he made sounds which may be definitely considered as musical, as distinguished from ordinary speech. He has always possessed a natural musical instrument. All the manufactured musical instruments necessarily came after his own instrument.

The subjective man

This fact gives the choral director much to think about. It means that the subjective side of Man, the emotions emanating from him, are audibly and directly expressed by his own vocal organ. To use an instrument for playing such sounds is the secondary way of expressing the feelings. This brings into use an intermediary article of some sort. Any instrument thereby becomes an agency second to the voice itself, which is primary. Inflections and intensities of the musical outpourings are naturally limited by the instrument. The human voice is not so limited, being limited in range only. Great joy, grief, longing, satisfaction and similar emotions can be best expressed by the direct connection of the voice physically with the person himself. Keeping this in mind one comes to the realization that the only way for the human being to subjectively express what is in his heart is by the use of his own vocal organ. How a great actor can move audiences by the pathos or fire suggested by the proper inflection of one single word! How the great orators of former days could work on the emotions of millions! How the great singers have learned to express their whole soul through the medium of the voice! No manufactured instrument can even approach this *personal* instrument.

Psychic influence

The choral director, therefore, has the advantage of the instrumentalist. He has a group of human beings, all with varying feelings and emotions, the result of hundreds of years of heredity and environment. His mission is to give them musical expression of this total combination. If he does it well, his singers will, perhaps without being conscious of it, pour out these feelings and emotions as they could not do with any set of instruments, even though they be expert players. When singing in such bodies or groups, such a feeling of union with the Invisible and of *esprit de corps* among themselves will develop that real comradeship is apparent. In fact, a well trained choral body that has been singing together for years will often do their numbers without the aid of a conductor. It is a matter of common observation that smaller groups, such as male quartets, develop such a unity of feeling, that a conductor is unnecessary and in many cases would be a hindrance. Large choirs that have this unity of feeling will often disregard the director's signal for an attack and wait perhaps several seconds before that telepathic current is shot through the group, causing them to begin as one person! This is not theory. It actually happens with the great choirs of the world.

Aesthetics in the body of singers is therefore apparent in the mutual outpourings of the heart and the stirrings of the emotions until a realization of the beautiful is made more personal, whether that be due to the text of the song or to the pure beauty of the blended sounds.

The listener

The beautiful side of it all is not confined to the singers. Those who listen cannot fail to realize the supreme beauty of human voices, well blended. There are three kinds of such tones and each has a different aesthetic effect on the audience. The choral conductor who would develop any one of these types should decide, before he begins, which he prefers.

The child tone

First, there is the tonal-type of the children's group. Until the age of adolescence the child voice consists almost solely of overtones or partials. That is to say, the full solid tone of the adult is not present either in quality or in actual physical make-up. Without going into a scientific discussion here, it should suffice to say that all tone is the product of a fundamental vibrating medium which produces, of itself, one foundation tone. Superimposed on this fundamental tone is a whole series of other tones called overtones or partials which are in a direct mathematical ratio of vibration to the main tone. The child voice does not have this fundamental tone. It is similar to a brass horn which is built in the manufacturer's work shop from the natural series of partials of a tone or set of tones. The fundamental tone is almost impossible to play on the average horn-family instrument.

Partials present

From my own observation, I am convinced that the child voice is not made up of the first octave partial but rather from the second overtone, the fifth. When a child sings C above middle C the main tone generating this tone is not middle C, but F below that C. This is what imparts to the well placed child voice the unearthly beauty of a clear blue sky. It also produces a voice penetrating and unpleasant when it is allowed to be used with pressure. The fifth is the most penetrating of the partials (see Helmholtz—"Sensations of Tone") and at the same time it is the most beautiful when in exact relation mathematically to its fundamental. Perhaps this is the reason why children, during infancy, produce such piercing tones. Tones completely out of the reach of an adult are sung by infants in the course of their ordinary cries.

Apparent dissonance

When listening to children sing with an orchestral accompaniment, occasionally there is heard an apparent dissonance (discord) with certain progressions of the orchestra. This is due to the fact that in passing that particular node of vibration, the voices, with their resultant tone, are not always in true vibration ratio to the instrumental combination tone. As the age of the singer increases this disappears and in adult life is scarcely noticeable.

Adolescent tones

The second tone-type is distinct from the tone of children and from the adult tone. It is the tone given forth by the adolescent of high school and college age. Its beauty tends to disappear when the voice becomes "changed." This, of course, is due to the physical changes taking place throughout the anatomy and is dependent directly on the sex change. The adolescent chorus can move audiences to tears. An audience is not conscious of the reason for its deeply stirred emotions when hearing certain chords sung by the adolescent chorus. This is because we have here a motley blending, as it were, of the child's fifth overtone with the adolescent first octave overtone. Those voices which are the most changed bring out the first octave. Those the least changed bring out the fifths. On the other hand, if this tone is not produced smoothly and evenly, we have a "cutting" tone which is often described as "going right through the head of the listener." High school choruses which sing harshly cause excruciating nerve-convulsions for the listener; but when controlled or well placed singing occurs, the result is so beautiful that all the color and warmth of tropical islands seem to emanate.

Adult tones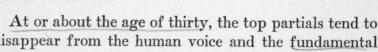

At or about the age of thirty, the top partials tend to disappear from the human voice and the fundamental tone becomes more prominent. Adult choruses composed of singers above this age are colorless and often described as uninteresting. Great singers, such as were Melba and Schumann-Heink, are much in the minority after this age. Those who succeed, as they did, in keeping the lustre of the voice to the age of fifty, are those who, for certain anatomical reasons, have not lost the overtones which were so prominent in youth. An adult chorus, from the standpoint of the conductor and the listener, is very uninteresting unless there be in that chorus a liberal sprinkling of younger people who will furnish the much needed color of tone.

CHAPTER II

EDUCATIONAL VALUES OF CHORAL MUSIC (THE GRADES)

Mass education

Today we are engaged in a gigantic task of educating the masses. Originally education was confined to the individual. It is only within the last century that mass education has come to actual employment at the hands of educators. Even after the European movements of revolution and after the American separation from the mother country the germ of individual education was still rampant. Brotherhood, equality of man, liberty, fraternity, state control, communism and all the other characteristics of the growing mass-consciousness created a field for educators.

Sight reading

At the earliest possible moment sight reading should be begun. I am not sure but that it could be introduced in kindergarten. This could be accomplished by naming the Do the "stop-tone" or the "red-light" tone, meaning "to stop" or "come to rest". The Ti (which is the most important of all) could be called the "green light" tone, meaning "to go ahead". In fact from Ti one *must* go

9

ahead to some other point. An ingenious kindergarten teacher who is musical can invent ways of teaching all of these syllables from their *sound* which is the all-important thing about them. There is no logical reason why sight reading should be left until the third or fourth grade. On leaving the kindergarten for the grades the pupil should be given a little book with large notes in it. Without knowing whether these notes were F, or G, or B-flat, or any other particular name, he should learn to associate a few notes at a time with certain syllables which he has learned in kindergarten. His musical reading process should be the same as the English reading process. Children learn to read whole words before they can spell them. Why not learn the musical phrases and syllables in the same way? If not ready for books let the music supervisor place one or two such phrases as "La-Ti-Do" on the blackboard and leave them there for a time. The child will learn this sequence by association with it in this manner.

Natural sight reading

Sight reading as it is often brought into play in the third or fourth grade is entirely like a mathematical table and the child learns to detest it. When it is brought into usage, regardless of the grade, it should be by association. The pupil learns to read the notes, going up and down, from their *position,* but not especially because they occupy any particular line or space. Lines and spaces should be left out of discussion and the child should be taught to read the notes by their *position* in progressing, either tone at a time (diatonically) or by intervals. Intervals should be the same size for several lessons. The lessons should be short. It is even possible to establish games in these grades, whereby the singing of the intervals may be embodied. When sight reading is thus made a part of daily association, such as is reading, a higher grade and the high school will not find so many entrants who cannot *yet* read music. This situation is all too realistic for any person in music education to ignore.

Choral music adapts to the idea

In truth it may be said that choral singing is the most elemental mass musical education that can be discovered. In a chorus the singers are all on the same plane. The good sight reader is indistinguishable from the poor sight reader. The soloist is not in evidence. In an opera or operetta the cast is the main thing. In choral programs the chorus is the main thing. Therefore the music educator should concentrate on mass choral singing if he wishes to be in line vocally with the modern idea of education. Only in proportion to the mass education done now will the future choral societies thrive. Only in proportion to the choral work done in the schools now will the adult generation have a definite love for choral music. Participation actively as an individual with a mass of other individuals is far better than sitting on the side-lines and listening. This kind of person never gets beyond the stage of wishing to pay his good money to hear someone else do the work. American publics are rather prone to support symphony orchestras, opera companies and artist courses, when, in addition to these very worthy activities, they should be taking part in musical events. We should not become a nation of absorbent listeners but rather one of active participants. Choral training will eventually produce this condition. It will prove to be the salvation of the American musical life.

The idea in elementary schools

The conductor's first field of endeavor is his contact with the child fresh from the home. From kindergarten to seventh grade there are seven years of formative period. Songs are developed from rote procedure, that is, the teacher sings the song phrase by phrase and the pupils imitate. Simple songs that have to do with the actual experiences of the child up to this point are advisable. For example, Mother Goose rhymes which are usually well known by little children can come into play in the kindergarten, set to melodies of simple structure. Then songs dealing with such subjects as the robin red breast, the sky, the trees, the dog, the cat, the postman, and the policeman find ready expression through melodic conveyance. These songs may be described as those having a personal reaction from the child to the subject about which he is singing.

The first three years

Care and discrimination should be used for kindergarten and the first two grades. Many teachers select songs dealing with the amusing and witty sayings of children because they are "cute," assuming that the children will revel in singing them. Child psychologists have discovered many things. Chief of them is the fact that children at this age are self centered and apt to talk about what they themselves are doing and thinking. In conversation they talk of what "I" am going to do or what "my father thinks," and various similar subjects. But while self centered in this respect the child psychologists have not brought out that a child in song is exactly the opposite. Therefore we find the child singing with great enthusiasm about the bird or the flower or the various things which have to do with his growing contact with the outside world. If a "cute" song is given him embodying some of the witty remarks of clever children his interest falls dead. This is a marked proof that song provides a channel for personal expression without actually talking about the person. The contact of that person with the universe and his soul-reaction to it are best expressed in group singing. Often these "cute" songs are what some adult composer *thinks* are amusing to children, whereas they are amusing things that children bring about for adults to be regaled with, but they are not funny at all to the children themselves. In fact the singing of such songs will tend to make the child draw up within himself to prevent his being laughed at. There are several volumes of just such songs. They are indeed beautiful little songs and very amusing to adults. They should be sung by an adult artist for adult audiences. The giving of these songs to kindergarten and early grade pupils is a mistake.

Songs of this period should embrace only those sentiments which have to do with actual *things* with which he is coming into contact every day. If he does not live in mountainous country it is foolish to have him sing a song about mountains. If he has never seen the sea and heard its waves, songs describing such beauties are barren to him. But if he has seen a parade and finds a song about a parade and its animals, just watch him love that song. All dogs are alike and so are birds to a child of this age. Just personify a dog or a bird and have the child sing what the bird or dog does or thinks and watch him get interested!

The second three years

Above the third grade and until the seventh, two-part songs are to be recommended. Three-part songs may be sung, but it is problematical as to the efficacy of this treatment. The main reason is that, as stated earlier, changes are constantly taking place and a wide range of voices is impossible. Altos and sopranos have about the same range, their difference being one of quality. Therefore the two-part song should be taught to the whole room or chorus. That is to say, each singer should learn both parts and on one occasion let half of the group sing the soprano and the other half the alto. On another occasion reverse the position.

Discovery of an outstanding alto during these grade years means that the child has lapsed into a guttural way of singing and, instead of being elated, the teacher should attempt to correct the defect.

The subject matter of these songs can gradually become changed as the child learns more about life and the world from his own associations. Eventually the child procedure can be forgotten as subject matter is concerned. Small cantatas such as settings of famous poems may now be introduced. As the upper grades are approached, this connection with the English materials should be made. It not only pleases those in authority in the school and the English teacher, but it is good educational practice. Make contact with other lines of study wherever possible.

Tone quality

The grades contain the new voices. They will be improved or harmed according to the method used in production of tone at this age. Children in kindergarten and the lower grades should not be allowed to sing from the throat, regardless of how much tone-volume the supervisor may wish to get from the chorus. The high tone, sung with open head, and rightly placed by the teacher, will be imitated faithfully by the children. Child groups which sing with hard tone are often the result of the teacher's own hard tone. Imitation is one of the strong characteristics of the formative period. Let the teacher discard the adult voice and sing falsetto or *sotto voce,* if necessary, for the children's sake. Use the vowel "oh" very frequently and the head voice will become greatly improved. "Ah" is not a suitable vowel for production of good child-tone because it opens the throat at the base of the tongue and generally results in a throaty or strident tone. Many exercises are contained in books of instruction for children of this age in which the syllable "La" is used as a medium of singing. This should be changed to "Lo". The "oh" sound will greatly develop the fifth partial in the child voice and result in a beautiful choral tone by the time the sixth grade is reached.

The use of "oo" (as in moon) is good to secure more resonance, but the soft singing of "oo" exclusively, as is the practice in many schools, will produce beautiful tones, tones which, however, lack *strength*. It is safe to use "oo" *part of the time*.

The boy in the grades

This procedure must be particularly enforced with regard to the boys, for they are inclined to get enthusiastic and to begin to "yell" just for the fun of it. The critical age for boys is difficult to determine. When they reach eleven years of age the teacher should keep a sharp watch of them. After this age a general physical condition may start to develop overnight. A boy who is a high, clear soprano one day will sing the same tones with effort the next day. When effort occurs in a boy's singing, he should be carefully nursed with the singing of vowels in head voice or he should be allowed to remain silent for a whole year, if necessary.

I am not one of that school which holds that voices of boys may be put down gradually onto alto and tenor parts as the voice changes. Much damage is done by singing at all during this period. The changes are taking place here and to use the voice at all is like breaking a young colt into heavy harness work. If he can produce falsetto tones and still sing high soprano, it is much better than to put him down on alto. If he *must* be placed on some part, let it be the *lowest* part obtainable. This will help the change physically and will eventually develop a tenor or bass of good quality. To put him on the part next lowest to soprano will tend to hold back the voice change, when it should be accelerated, if anything. See page 53.

Boy sopranos and altos

There is no doubt but that there are definitely sopranos and altos among the boys, in the same manner as there are among the girls. The difference is one of quality, not of range. If the voice is bright and "silvery" it is undoubtedly soprano and *will become tenor when changed*. If the voice is more mellow and rich, inclined to be "golden", it is probably alto and *will become bass when changed*. Boy sopranos and altos can sing the same notes as the girl sopranos and altos and may be incorporated into two and three part music, singing regular SSA arrangements.

Boy voice groupings

It is a mistake to assume that because boys often insist on singing on low tones, even growling on an indiscriminate pitch, that they are low altos, tenors, or baritones and must be herded into one group or class called baritone, so that SAB arrangements can be used with them. The reason why these boys do not sing out and use the voice in proper range and quality is that they do not yet know how to *use* their voices. It is a common observation that many teachers are glad to get through a lesson period and call it "another day" rather than to take the time and the trouble to work with these boys and to develop them into good singers. The fact must be borne in mind that they can sing as well and as high and as low as the girls. Divide them accordingly and abandon the practice of considering boys' voices a necessary evil.

Monotones

There is no such thing as a true monotone. In years of experimental observation of this phenomenon called "monotonism", I have yet to see the boy's (or girl's) voice that will not respond to treatment and eventually sing the part correctly. It is true that many voices at first will not even match a tone played or sung for them. The problem is to find their *own* tone. Sing or play down to the tone which the singer is making and stay there with him a while, assuring and reassuring the singer that he has a good voice and can really sing the tone the teacher is singing or playing. Monotonism is another form of self-consciousness, as is also stuttering. The singer is often an introvert or afflicted with a nervous tension caused by some former illness or distorted concept. *The teacher's first task is to build confidence.*

From there on, various devices can be used, such as the well-known one of walking up the stairs a step at a time and singing a higher note each time. It takes work and it takes time out of class very often. In class the singer can be left to himself. Even though he gets out a book and studies his lesson in arithmetic while the class is singing, he will surely and slowly be "inoculated" with musical pitch senses all around him. In a regularly singing glee club, or singing class he should be placed near the part which he should be singing so that he can hear the changes of pitch in that part. In unison singing he should be encouraged to listen rather than to sing. Such patients require varying degrees of time in which to effect improvement. Some will respond in two or three weeks of every day work; others take months. Eventually, if the teacher is earnest, kindly and really interested, and if the singer *feels* this interest in him, he will certainly begin to emerge from his phobia or fixation, and will find that he *can* sing a part correctly.

In this discussion no mention is made of boys who like to growl in the depths just because they consider music quite feminine. This, and other attributes of boys, which many people fear and announce themselves as baffled about, often cause them to be considered monotones or basses "in the rough", as it were. Since this is not the result of any nervous disorder and thus can easily be handled, the previous discussion of monotonism applies only to such cases as are at first *beyond the control* of the prospective singer. Local disruptive influences are trivial and easily handled and thus are not worthy of discussion.

The teacher, in all cases, must remember that he is dealing with human beings and that, aside from his purely informative processes, he must also get into the heart of the pupil, make him like and admire his teacher and arouse a desire to show the teacher his appreciation of and belief in him. In any or all tactics used, the teacher must never, if it can be helped, let the word "monotone" be used or any other expression which will give the pupil a feeling of inferiority. He has this feeling already. It must first be ignored while he is treated as if he were a quite normal, even above-normal, human being. He must not even be called a "special case", and the word "corrective" should be avoided. Let the approach be casual, jolly and warm-hearted. Utter some such short remark as "Come on Bill, let's work on that voice of yours a bit. It's really a good one and I want to use you as one of my main singers—all you need is a little coaching, just like that swimmer you were telling me about". After all said in books, in lectures and in education classes, the teaching process comes back to the main thing, which is that the teacher who is a teacher, who feels it in his very soul that he *must* show others how to learn, is the teacher who is a humanized, personalized mental comrade of the pupil. He must have a genuine *love* for humanity, as humanity, and for individuals as if they were his own product whom he is interested in helping along the way through life.

CHAPTER III

EDUCATIONAL VALUES (JUNIOR HIGH SCHOOL)

Much has been said and written about the junior high school and its place in general educational procedure and method. The division of eight grades of grammar school and four grades of high school has not worked out so well, for the reason that the two higher grades of the lower school and the lowest grade of the high school constitute a peculiar type of child. This child is not a little child any longer; neither is he the older adolescent type. To mix him with grammar grades gives him a superficial sense of his own importance and to mix him with the high grades gives him an inferiority complex. Educators, with this in mind, have recommended and put into practice in most sections of the country, a combining of these grades into what is known as the junior high school.

The SAB arrangement

For musical development this has been a fortunate occurrence in some ways but more unfortunate in other ways. The fortunate part of it is due to the fact that the ages are similar and the active changing process going forward produces more similarity of vocal material. Seventh and eighth grade pupils no longer are compelled to work along with the younger children on the production of grade school cantatas and playlets. At the same time the freshman in high school does not have to wait a year or so before he is able to mix musically with the older high school people. This group, now combined, gives the musical coach a group that is very similar in mental characteristics and type of voices. In this sense the junior high school arrangement is fortunate for the music teacher.

The unfortunate part of the combination is that adequate material for this group has not been produced. The most frequently used type of music for the group has been the so-called SAB arrangement; an arrangement providing for two unchanged voice parts, soprano and alto, and for a third nondescript voice in the process of changing, called a baritone. This arrangement of music is detestable and should be discouraged and abandoned at the earliest opportunity. Proponents of this type of SAB music have argued that the boys are neither tenors nor basses and that they should have music arranged for them which will allow them all to sing one part, while the girls sing the soprano and alto parts.

Illogical aspect of the SAB arrangement

These friends of SAB music are in error. The fact is that the boys are very decidedly tenors or basses according to the *quality* of their voices. Right at this period they will be permanently harmed by being herded into one class called baritone. Here they are called upon to sing a very small range of tones. Those who are going to be good basses and those who will likewise become tenors, must then merge their voices in ONE part. It would be just as sensible to combine sopranos and altos into one limited part and call it "mezzo." The two qualities do not merge nor blend on the same part. They were not intended by Nature to do so. They blend when they are in their proper range and have proper vowel qualities on separate parts. They then adhere to the actual mathematical ratio of related vibrations.

The solution

What then is the answer to this question? A happy solution is to divide the singers into both tenor and bass sections, and to teach the tenors to sing their tones as lightly and as well as they can while the basses are learning to develop their voices on proper bass quality vowels and to read the bass clef. Tenors today generally read the treble clef and practically all choral music is so written. Why should these new tenors be compelled to sing with a great many basses on a part utterly unsuited to them and in a clef which they will not use when they ultimately become changed tenors? In addition to this is the fact that many of the so-called baritone parts are written too high for the basses. We have them taking the high tones in a strained voice and marring the beauty of the lighter tenor voices which may be singing in what is a proper range for them.

Quality versus range

The usual argument against this is that no one can distinguish the tenors from the basses—that they are all baritones. Such a statement proves that those who are placing the voices where they belong have been accustomed to choosing the voices according to how high or low they can sing, instead of by the quality of the voice. A music teacher with an ordinary ear can distinguish immediately a lighter head voice from a darker chest voice. These two voices may not be able to sing higher or lower than the other, but they do have decidedly different qualities. Our American public usually thinks of tenors and basses in terms of the range. This is a fallacy. They should be trained to think in terms of how light or how dark is the voice; the range is the result of the training in that particular color of voice. The range does not cause the voice; the voice causes the ultimate range! Music teachers in the junior high school will therefore do well to give attention to the color of the voice and let the range take care of itself as the voice grows. Only recently have educators realized that SAB music is not solving the problem of the disposition of boys in junior high school.

Junior high school mixed chorus

The proper music for junior high school mixed chorus is standard four-part music, SATB. This gives each kind of voice its chance to develop properly and to learn to blend with the whole ensemble in the proper manner.

On reaching senior high school the preliminary choral work has then been materially strengthened and the boys, as well as the girls, move on into senior high school music without undergoing another convolution of educational procedure.

Examples of material

The question, "What kind of four-part music?" now presents itself. It must be frankly stated that four-part songs which have short ranges for tenors and basses are fairly plentiful and many such numbers can be obtained by writing to the various publishers of good octavo music, describing what is desired. As a type of such music Gevaert's "The Sleep of the Child Jesus" is satisfactory. There is an adequate version of this number in the Witmark edition. The style of the composition calls for softly placed tones, sung without effort and sustained. The speed is slow enough to enjoy the harmonic progressions. There is no opportunity to sing loud or with forced tones, even though the group were struggling on the leash of pent-up enthusiasm. The intervals which occur are such as offer wonderful opportunity for the study of intonation, or how to keep on the pitch. It adapts itself to singing by syllables, *which method of learning to sight read is as good as any yet devised!*

But since four-part mixed choral music is often feared by the teacher, it may be that a more gradual approach to such music in the junior high school grades may be attained by developing parts and voices even from unison songs. Two parts, or those embodying descant can be used. Many teachers use a good unison chorus up until the final five or six chords and then teach some good harmonic progressions to be used as an ending. Often these chords employ up to eight parts and produce some thrilling effects for the chorus. An example of this is my own "Ode to the Homeland". While written originally as a unison chorus, the four part harmony is given to be used if desired. It can be sung in two parts only, or in three parts only. It can be experimented with by having the boys sing half a verse in unison and follow with the girls singing the remainder of the verse in unison, all joining in unison on the chorus. At the end comes the series of chords which serve excellently in training the harmonic sense. It is not going beyond the bounds of reason to say that *any* chorus from kindergarten to senior high school can sing such a chorus.

Another example is "A Scotch Christmas Carol", arranged for SSA by Lamont (Kjos edition). In the key in which this is arranged, the three parts may be sung in junior high school grades with both boys and girls singing the notes as written. If there are some changed voices of limited range which are bass or baritone, they can be told to sing the low notes of the left-hand piano part, thus making a simple four part number. If the number is to be used with girls alone or with boys alone it is often effective when done in a key a step or so higher up. The piano accompaniment may be transposed or written out higher, probably by one of the students who will have fun doing it.

Another example is Mozart's "Ave Verum", a well known number, sung and arranged in editions without number. As it occurs in the Ditson edition for SSA, the teacher will have a very effective number by lowering the pitch a bit and having all the boys sing the *melody* while the sopranos sing the second soprano part and the altos sing the alto part. The boys with unchanged voices will sing this melody as written *and the changed voices one octave lower,* while the girls sing as written. The effect, with the piano accompaniment provided, is positively enchanting. Another way to sing it is to have the four part chorus ready, regular SATB people. Take the SSA arrangement and let the sopranos sing the top part as written, the altos the second soprano part as written, the tenor boys and girls (low altos) sing the alto part as written and let the basses and baritones sing the bass notes of the piano left-hand part. Since this is not written out for singing, as a part, the teacher will have to point out the notes to be sung by the boys. This they will like, and they will have added zest in finding some notes which they are to sing to make up a four part version.

Other examples of very good music for four part junior high school choruses—numbers which may be sung, either four part as written, or in varying combinations, depending on the teacher's material and ingenuity: "Song of America" Southey (Summy edition), Down the Open Road (Haney) (B. F. Wood edition), Ave Verum (Des Pres) (Flammer edition), In the Merry Spring (Ravenscroft) (Witmark edition), If My Songs Had Wings (Hahn) (Hall McCreary edition) and others of similar range and adaptability by the dozen.

What is the procedure in finding and using such material? Simply one of not being confined to SAB music and its restrictive influences. The teacher, to be true, must, of course, use some inventiveness; in many cases "doctoring" or transposing numbers which need it, but the choice of material should lie with the usability of it, the attractiveness of it to the singers, the inspiration which is gotten out of it, and its good quality. The *printed* notes and ranges should be considered last, because they can always be adapted to the singers, or the singers to them. The main point is that four part to eight part music should be sung. And it should be *good* music, good literature, both in notes and in words, with which the young chorus singer is thus prepared for his way on up into senior high schools.

Effect of good material

After all is said along other lines, the fact remains that this is good music and after learning it, the junior high school chorus will have much higher respect for the teacher than after the singing of the usual cheap type of song. Our students today should be given material to learn to sing which is on a par, in difficulty, with their English and mathematics. *The "learning process" as*

*applied to such good music will result in the instillment
of permanent cultural values!*

Junior high school girls' and boys' glee clubs

For junior high school girls' glee clubs the three-part repertoire is to be recommended. There is an unlimited supply of such music. For boys' choruses there are a few two and three-part numbers and the supply is being rapidly increased. The ranges of the boys are so limited that the best arrangements leave much to be desired.

The possibilities of boys' choruses are tremendous here since the teacher has boy sopranos and altos along with tenors and basses. Of course such choruses will not sing TTBB arrangements but instead will devote themselves to regular SATB arrangements, being in effect a mixed choir. Boy's choruses singing SATB music are tremendously effective. The mistake has often been made of trying to use four part male chorus music here, in TTBB arrangement, allowing the boy sopranos and altos to sing the top parts an octave higher than the changed-voice tenors would sing. This produces an uncanny effect and one which is decidedly stilted. It seems beyond the bounds of good judgment that a teacher should think that because he has a boys' chorus it should sing only TTBB music, when he is cognizant at the same time that the two top parts must be sung an octave higher! If TTBB music is used (and this, I think would indeed be rare in junior high grades except in sections of the country where the boys are larger and older)—if TTBB music is used at all, it should be sung in the same pitch as adult men would sing it. For real boy-chorus singing, using SATB or TTBB music, the old masters themselves wrote most of such music. And in America today, we now have some very splendid boy choruses in junior high schools. It is begging the point to say that it can't be done. It just simply is done with ordinary boys! And, since boys are the same everywhere, it can be done everywhere if they can be gotten together for a rehearsal and then given some music to sing, well taught and inspiringly led.

Tone quality in the junior high school

During the age of the junior high school pupil, the tone quality of the voices is beginning to develop the first overtone combined with the second, but the first more predominant. Since the voices are more mature than in early grades, the tonal broadening can now be begun by using the vocal "oh" with mouth open and lower jaw down and as relaxed as possible. Let the sound be as though coming from a resonant chamber. If there is difficulty in communicating the idea to the students let them feel as open and as free as though they were going to make a very hollow and roaring hooting or "booing" sound. This sound *can* be made from the throat but it will lack the roaring characteristics if made from the throat and is easily ascertainable. Develop this tone on any word that comes along in the text which contains the vowel "o"; for example "home". If there is not a chord at this point in the music, give the various divisions of the chorus a note to sing in a chord. Let them practice holding and singing this chord first with just "oh". Then transfer the "oh" tone into words like "land", "sing", "dream" and others until the vowels of all the other words are broadened and darkened by the use of the "oh". It is better to exaggerate and overdo the covering and darkening of the tone at this age, than correct the tone quality later on by allowing the singers to brighten and sharpen the tone. The speaking voice is so likely to be flat, nasal and throaty at this age, that a counter effective dose of the broad round tone will be what is needed. The chorus, if trained in this way will develop a very resonant diapason organ tone, similar to mellow yet resonant brass.

In developing tone, as such, and purely as such, the naturalness of pronunciation will somewhat suffer at first. The word "God", for instance, will sound more like "Goad" than "Gawd". "Land" will sound more like "Loaned" than "Laand". But as experimentation increases and as the singers learn first how to shape their mouths and to place tones in the middle of the head and away from the throat, the naturalness of the pronunciation will improve. It goes without saying that the *speaking* voice of all pupils of this age and older is a very important factor in the kind of singing voice they will use. More attention should be paid to the development of a pleasing resonant, un-strident speaking voice, well modulated at all times. Teachers of musical groups would do well to familiarize themselves with a course in speech, and learn how to teach their own pupils the proper use of the speaking voice. The best singers, actors and speakers that have ever appeared on the musical horizon have been so trained. Results speak for themselves. For further study of this point refer to the drawings of the head cavities with placement of vowels shown.

CHAPTER IV

EDUCATIONAL VALUES (SENIOR HIGH SCHOOL)

The adolescent here comes into his own. Emerging from the preparatory years of the correctly-taught junior high school chorus we find singers entering the senior high school chorus with properly placed tones, a limited knowledge of the beauty of the four-part singing and a desire to further develop into more than four-part work. There is also a liberal addition of male choruses which have by this time more possibilities as to employment of ranges.

The chorus

Three-part songs still offer the most effective material for the girls while the boys may sing four-part songs. It is generally more satisfactory, however, to concentrate on the large chorus of both boys and girls in from four to eight parts, because of the greater possibilities culturally as well as musically. There is, to begin with, a greater number of available compositions for such choruses. When once learned, any of the Italian, Tudor, German, English, modern English, Russian and American schools of composition offer keen enjoyment to the young singers of high school ages. The ranges in places will still be rather more extended than many of the singers can manipulate, but the overlapping of parts and the possibilities of substitution on parts or notes for parts which are weak will serve to bring about the same result musically and culturally. Added to this is the fact that only an adolescent chorus can sing such music with the pure beauty which the composer had in mind. The Russians have given the most colorful things to the choral world. Gretchaninoff's "Autumn", "Sun and Moon", Rachmaninoff's "Ave Maria" and the "Znamen Traditional Melody" form the easier type, while progress may be made from these to the larger works as they are presented. The works of Palestrina, Vittoria, Lotti, and others of the old Italian school as well as Tomkins, Wm. Byrd, Purcell, Morley, and others representing well the old English school can be studied without overtaxing the powers of the chorus.

It must be kept in mind that the average high school student is capable of far more than is popularly supposed. There is more danger in underestimating the abilities of these keen-minded modern youngsters than there is in overtaxing them. Those who would attempt the modern English school are recommended to the works of Gustav Holst, Vaughn Williams, Cyril Jenkins, Arnold Bax and Arthur Benjamin. These people all know how to write for the choral group and the effects they produce aesthetically are tremendous.

Should the oratorio be given?

The oratorio is not to be recommended to high school choruses. Certain excerpts such as "He Shall give His Angels charge over Thee" from "Elijah" are very good because they do not overtax the actual physical endurance of the young vocal cords. Handel's "Messiah" should seldom be sung by young people in high school, because it is primarily a mature adult work, written for adults or of such settled voices that the long rehearsals necessary to execute the florid runs will not wear them out.

Exception must here be made and attention called to *The Messiah* as revised for adolescent voices by Richard Kountz (Witmark), a revision accomplished not by melodic distortion, nor even by change of key, but by the re-allocating of individual parts (never less than a complete musical phrase) so that the melodic line is always within easy range. This treatment tends ever to more closely knit (as against a more widely dispersed) tonal structure and, in that sense at least, moves in the direction of *strength*. Since the educational and cultural advantages to adolescents resulting from singing this great oratorio may thus be gained without vocal damage, this revised edition is recommended to the reader's attention.

The "Hallelujah" chorus is perhaps the least taxing physically of any of the "Messiah" choruses. There is no necessity for the concentration of high school choruses on long and overwrought oratorios, with their continual demands for power and climaxes. Tones of such choruses will eventually become hard and unpleasant. The wise supervisor would rather busy himself with a development of his chorus for excellence in tone quality and the wider experience of the various pure vocal schools, than to prepare his chorus for the singing of an oratorio in an effort to show proud principals and doting parents what kind of "stunts" his singers can do. Of course they can do it! No one questions that; but in what shape does it leave their voices from year to year? And again, how much do they know of the entire repertoire of the beautiful choral schools? It is rather to be compared to an English teacher who teaches her classes nothing but Shakespeare's plays.

Should opera or operetta be given?

Choruses in operas and operettas do not demand the continued tension that oratorio choruses demand. The chorus in an operetta is secondary to the cast, and therefore has very little to sing compared with the oratorio. Vocally, many operatic choruses can be sung by high school choruses without doing permanent harm to the voices.

The question then is not so much whether the works can be given vocally as it is whether their educational value warrants their use. It would seem to be entirely logical to teach that which most perfectly conforms to sound educational practice. The operatic performance does not fulfill the educational requirements. It is not in keeping at all with the theory of mass education, because only a favored few, those with the best voices, are allowed to sing the "leads" while the chorus furnishes the background. In this most essential requisite for choral education the opera and operetta are lacking!

Again, the operatic production is recreational as an end in itself. True musical education follows more closely the cultural values which can be gained only from some kind of musical study which will develop the mind, rather than the box office receipts or the adulation of the school. Geometry would be discarded from all curricula if its "appeal" and its "tinsel" and "glory" were considered as the main function of its relation to the student body. Opposition to the giving of operettas is not intended in this opinion. Such entertainments undoubtedly have their place in the school life, but the suggestion is here offered that there is a lack of real music education in a choral development of operas and operettas if it results in a lessening of other forms of choral music.

It would appear that the singing of choruses either accompanied or *a cappella,* choruses designed for choral technique and display as well as for appeal, choruses not overly "arranged" or distorted from an old master, choruses without extraction from some score or arranged from a piano piece, choruses with due attention to all the choral literature of the last five centuries, these, both sacred and secular, and all taken together, would be the ideal choral education for the American youth.

This kind of education fulfills the first requisite, namely, that it is group education! It is not the education of soloists or of operatic casts. The chorus is the important consideration, not the selected few. Here are good soloists, poor soloists, good sight readers, poor sight readers, wealthy talented students, poor aspiring students all blended in one assimilative mass bent on expressing themselves through choral tone and the beauty of the spiritual appeal which dates back to primitive man.

On the stage, especially if the chorus wears vestments or uniforms of some sort, there is no distinction between individual singers. It is the group! Long live the group, the mass! It is the salvation of our future American singing adult life and it will eventually remake the nation into one of singing participants rather than one of passive enjoyers.

The "hold-over" feature

The chorus fulfills the second requisite, namely, that it presupposes and develops culture and cultural values which will hold over into adult life. It is not recreational as an end in itself. The chorus does not sing for the "fun" of it until after the long and tedious hours of rehearsal are over and the whole body of singers can blend in a lift of song from the heart to the Invisible. Then the true recreational value asserts itself, identifying itself as the recreation of the mind and soul in reflection on things beautiful. This quality, much sought after as the aim of our curricula exposition, comes into its own and lasts into adult life. The proof of it is in the avidity with which the singers in choruses of high schools gravitate toward such choruses when they reach college. Again, when the college days are over, the adult in the community turns to his community chorus or choir. It gets into the blood. It becomes an obsession which cannot be satisfied with ordinary singing societies, community sings, minstrel shows, and alumni operettas. It goes far beyond superficial recreation and becomes an implanted characteristic of school days which blossoms forth with much fruition in adult life.

The spiritual development

Lastly, it satisfies the spiritual urge in adolescents as no other form of musical education can do. There is no such thing as religious education in public school systems and perhaps this is well in the light of our present-day heterogeneity of society. But the religious urge is there, nevertheless, in high school. It is stirred and fired by the sexuo-mental changes taking place. The person is most romantic at this age, and most ideal in his aspirations. To supply this expression of romantic tendency and religious appeal in a way that the soul can pour itself out, through participation in choral body-tone, is something that is greatly needed. In song this means of expression is found. It is primitive but it is personal. It is spiritual.

The a cappella style

For those who insist that there is no better music than the *a cappella* type of composition, it might be said that they can be excused for this addiction to beautiful music. But much that is *a cappella* is also very unworthy music. The point in beautiful choral singing is hardly whether or not the music is sung accompanied or unaccompanied, but rather that it is sung well and beautifully. There is an adequate supply of both kinds of choral material. To insist that no music is worth while unless it is *a cappella* is like saying that there is no branch of athletics except football. True, this is a highly organized branch of sport, but it does not constitute the *whole* of sport. As there are other branches of the same department let there be also many branches of the choral department. A well organized and equipped high school should have a large mixed chorus unrestricted as to membership; out of that should be selected perhaps a very expert smaller group called the *a cappella* choir, girls choruses, boys choruses, small ensembles of various sizes and perhaps even a special group for the giving of operettas only.

The really great *a cappella* music is still great. A choral society which concentrates exclusively on such music might be said to have attained a high degree of excellence, especially in learning to sing independently of any accompanying agency. Training in pitch perfection is, of course, much enhanced by the *a cappella* style. Every chorus should learn to sing unaccompanied as well as accompanied. But to say that the *a cappella* style forms the "highest" art in choral music is sheer nonsense.

The *a cappella* movement in the United States brought about great advancement in the singing technique of choirs. It raised the standard of material to be sung. It produced many other changes in educational procedure with the young singers. In fact, it went much too far in certain respects. Often a chorus is encountered which is singing a number *a cappella*—a number which was written with an accompaniment and of which the accompaniment is an integral part! A lullaby, for instance may definitely *need* the rocking-cradle accompaniment. A song of joy may perhaps be definitely identified with certain arpeggios in the accompaniment. Colorings of harmonies and addenda to the choral score are very much needed in many works of a specific type. To discard the accompaniment and to sing such a song *a cappella,* because it is supposed to be the "style" or the latest thing, is, of course, very lamentably lacking in both good taste and good sense. Teachers in contests often thus discard the accompaniment because they think that the judge will give them a higher rating if they show their independence of accompaniment. The judge, if he knows his business, will give them a lower rating for not singing the song the way it was designed and written, especially if the accompaniment is a figured and needed score and not merely a support of the voices. On the other hand it is, of course, not necessary to use an accompaniment which is of itself only a support to the voice parts, merely duplicating them in most cases. All in all, there is in the whole *a cappella* "movement" a need for common ordinary "horse sense" in dealing with choral problems.

CHAPTER V

THE PRACTICE OF CHORAL MUSIC

Since the chorus has been shown to most completely measure up to standard in point of aesthetics, and in educational procedure, the rest of this book will be devoted exclusively to a discussion of the functioning of this type of choir.

Preparation

The preparation of a chorus for rehearsal involves both physical and psychical factors. Among the physical factors are the place of rehearsal, time of rehearsal, seating arrangement, type of seats, procurement of music, uniforms, tests, officers and finances. Among the psychical factors are mental attitude of the conductor, type of music to be rehearsed, the weather and its effect and proper advance on the number to be sung.

Place of rehearsal

The kind of room in which a rehearsal is to be held is the first consideration. It will not suffice to take the prospective chorus into any room which is large enough to contain it. Unfortunately many choral conductors are compelled to hold their rehearsals in a room which has been selected for them with the size of the room in mind rather than the effect of the room.

Good ventilation *for Charles poam*

The room, first of all, should have means of adequate ventilation. In the process of singing, particularly if the action be vigorous, there is much bodily activity. Since it takes place within doors and with the bodies of singers confined to one set of seats or places until the rehearsal is over, it follows that all body poisons thrown off in breathing or through the pores of the body are not dissipated as they would be in the open air where there is freedom of action and ventilation. Absorption of these poisons is apt to be the result. The air becomes poisoned and fatigue of the singers thereby becomes a probability.

Lighting

The room should be well lighted from the back and sides and the singers should not face the light. If the rehearsal is to be held at night, the light should be directly over the singers but not in front of them. This means that the conductor will be placed at some disadvantage in his position facing the light, but either the conductor or the singers must be the victims of such annoyance. It is the conductor's duty to give his singers every advantage even at the expense of his own comfort.

Shape of room and acoustical properties

The shape of the rehearsal room is a predetermining factor in a good rehearsal. A room which is oval or semicircular is best for the proper blending of tones without echo. A long room which is proportionately narrow presents a problem. If the singers face the end of such a room, echoes and overtones will result. In order to counteract this tendency the conductor may force the tones of the chorus and unpleasant tone quality will result, which will not be noticed at the rehearsal. The conductor is later much surprised when, on taking the chorus to a concert hall or theater with good acoustical properties, the chorus displays a hard and unpleasant tone.

If the singers sit facing the side of such a long room there will develop much stridency of tone combined with a tendency to get off pitch. This is caused by the throwback of tone waves from the immediate side walls, and does not mean that the singers are forcing their tones, yet it sounds to the conductor as if they were. The conductor will probably spend much time combating this apparent stridency. When he appears in concert with such a chorus, particularly in a concert hall with good acoustical properties, the chorus will seem to exhibit undue weakness and lack of sonority. The conductor explains it by attributing it to nervousness or stage-fright.

If the conductor realizes that his singers are not really forcing tones in such a rehearsal room, but that they merely sound that way to him, such a room has an advantage, in that every defect of pitch or diction is magnified and the conductor, working on these defects, is able to produce a performance of much refinement. If the conductor, during rehearsal, subdues the tones of the chorus too much, they will appear weak when giving the concert, but the refinement and finesse developed may completely offset this loss of volume to the advantage of both chorus and conductor.

The ideal room

The best room is one which is almost square and with a high ceiling. Low ceiling in any type of room will prove to be a reflecting medium similar to the reflecting side of the long room just considered. If possible, a room should be secured which has a ceiling with arches or slopes upward toward a dome or peak. If they are not too spacious, such rooms usually have excellent acoustics. If the room is capable of seating more than six hundred people, the chances are that it will become an absorbing medium and constitute a hindrance rather than a help.

An auditorium with arched or vaulted roof, which will seat not more than four hundred people, and which is almost square is the ideal room.

Special walls and ceilings

Rooms which have a special preparation on walls and ceilings, designed to deaden or absorb the sound (such as is found in many band rehearsal rooms) are to be avoided for chorus rehearsal. The resonance so necessary to good intonation is totally lacking. Modern radio studios are now built with a movable wall, a large hinged panel or series of such panels being provided so that they may be swung back and the bare plaster wall exposed to the sound waves. By careful testing, the correct amount of bare wall can thus be exposed and the remainder of the wall blanketed.

The raised floor

Finally, in discussing the attributes of a good rehearsal room, the raised floor must not be overlooked. If there is no pitch or rise to the floor so that each row of seats is higher than the succeeding row, it will be worth the expense and the effort to bring about some such condition by altering the floor or by building up risers of a portable nature. Singers who rehearse, seated on the same level, do not give the results that may be obtained from those who rehearse on a raised floor. It is not sufficient to have the conductor raised on a platform or stage. It is not a question of seeing the conductor. *The prime purpose of the raised floor is to raise each succeeding row of singers so that the tone of one row will not be blanketed by the row in front of it.* Tone quality and resonance is increased by this simple expedient and often, when once raised, a chorus will sound entirely unlike its former self.

The seats, too, should be of the detachable type and not too comfortable. (The singers should not have seats that encourage them to slump down.) The conductor must, during rehearsal, walk in and out among the singers, listening to individual tones and noting peculiarities of tone quality and timbre. Benches or opera chairs which are fastened together make such action impossible and are not best for choral purpose. Let the chairs or rows of chairs be vertical as opposed to the conductor, so that he may have access to any point in the entire chorus by merely taking a few steps.

Time of rehearsal

Having selected a suitable place, the next important step is to select a proper time for the rehearsals. In schools where the program for rehearsal is set by the administration office there is not much choice in this matter and yet the conductor may so arrange with those who make out the schedule that the chorus rehearsals take place at an advantageous time.

A rehearsal which takes place early in the morning is not satisfactory. The voice improves as the day wears on, up to about an hour before sunset. There is then a drop of potential voice beauty and power until about an hour after sunset when the voice again improves and continues to attain brilliance and clarity as the evening progresses. It would seem best from these observations, to hold all rehearsals in the evening if it can be arranged.

If the rehearsal must be held during the day and in regular school hours, let it take place before lunch or at least one hour after lunch. Early in the morning the body is fresh physically but the voice lacks spirit. So much of singing is dependent on the spirito-nervous reaction. This side of the human being does not come to the fore until the purely physical exuberance has somewhat abated.

A rehearsal immediately after lunch puts an additional strain on the conductor, who must be ever alert in matters of sagging pitch and drooping spirits.

CHAPTER VI

ORGANIZING THE CHORUS

Selecting the singers

There are two methods of approach to this problem. When the conductor desires a small, mobile, selected group, the test will necessarily be more exacting and will contain such features as extended sight reading tests, ear tests, tone quality and intensity tests and other more particular tests.

When the conductor takes the large mass, just as it comes to him and determines to weld that mass into a good singing unit, his problems of selection are few. Viewed in the light of best educational procedure this method is more commendable. It is much more to any conductor's credit that he take all who come and have them sing from the best choral literature. His influence on the future citizenship of the individuals is multiplied by this attitude.

Some conductors find it possible to have both kinds of chorus. This makes possible a variety of digression into the realm of choral literature and perhaps makes the conductor's own life more interesting. The general plan of procedure in rehearsal with either type of chorus, once the singers have been selected, is the same.

Testing the mass chorus should progress after the following fashion: Let the candidate come to the piano and sing "oh" along with the tones that the conductor may play. The candidate does not know for what he is being tested and consequently soon relaxes. Three things are discovered in this simple test.

1. The tester will discover the candidate's ability to stay on the pitch or to follow a set series of pitches.
2. He will discover the range of the voice.
3. The quality, that is, whether it be soprano, alto, tenor or bass, will be ascertained.

Too much stress cannot be laid on the principle that the selection of and placing of a singer on any given part should not depend on his range, but on the quality of his tone.

It is assumed that during this simple test, the other candidates who are in the room will dispose themselves as they may wish, even talking and conversing pleasantly on various topics of the day. This is desirable and should not be discouraged or stopped by the teacher, because it provides a back-ground of noise behind which the timid candidate may hide himself while he sings his "oh's". His self consciousness is thus reduced to a minimum. He soon realizes that the whole company of candidates is not listening to him. The tester will further aid the candidate by requesting him to stand with his back to the others in the room.

The candidate should be placed in such a position

that he cannot see the keys of the piano. He should not know what tones he is singing, for he may have a preconceived idea of how high or how low he can sing.

The tester should have the candidate stand so that he does not look directly into the face of the tester. This reduces timidity and self consciousness, at the same time giving the tester an opportunity to notice the action of the jaw and throat while producing the tone. Many cases of deficiencies have been discovered in this way and a few cases of incipient goitre have been found and reported, to the subsequent good fortune of the singer.

The sight reading test

A sight reading test should not be given. This kind of test is very desirable for a highly selective chorus, but not for a general mass chorus. It has been demonstrated that general mass choruses have been able to produce thrilling effects in singing music that moves the heart, and yet not contain many sight readers. The natural process is that those who do read fairly well will take the leadership in rehearsals and that those who cannot read will follow. As time goes on these will become more proficient by the simple process of association with the notes. They will learn that when the notes rise on the printed page, the voice should rise, and that descending notes call for descending voice. Eventually they will learn just how far to go up and down, by the process of *visual fixation.* Many good sight readers have been developed in this way, who would never have been accepted into the chorus if they had been required to pass a sight reading test when entering!

The lack of sight reading ability will slow down the rehearsals, but, as the season progresses, the ground covered will increase. It is true that a great amount of such rehearsing is in effect learning "by ear," but no great criticism can be leveled at such learning. Why not learn by ear, since Music itself appeals through that very medium?

Test should start on a high tone

It is advisable to select, for test, a tone which is rather high in the vocal register of the average person. To begin with a low tone and proceed up-scale with the candidate following is not good, since the chest tone will thus be carried up high and real quality not discovered so easily. By starting on a high tone and proceeding downward, at the same time cautioning the candidate to sing softly, the head voice quality will more often assert itself and will carry down into the chest register.

The vowel "oo" (as in moon) is not advised as a test vowel. It has a tendency to close the throat and pinch the tone into the top of the head passages thus producing what is akin to falsetto! In such a procedure many a bass will sound like a tenor, and a contralto often will sing higher than a soprano, and they may be placed on the wrong part.

Balance

In selecting voices and placing them in the proper part, balance will usually take care of itself, since the human race is on the average the same for any given number of both sexes. Therefore, for a large mass group it will not be necessary to limit the number of any one part. Even among selected choruses of the adult type, tenors are fewer in proportion to basses, than are altos in proportion to sopranos. It even seems as though the Divine Creator made tenors a scarce article so that over-ambitious conductors would not put too many in choruses! Indeed, a few tenors will balance many times their number of basses. Their tones are more penetrating and higher in range.

For a selected choir which may wish to enter the realm of double choir music or even go so far as to sing the forty part motet of Tallis, "Spem in alium nunquam habui", it is advisable that there be at least 16 tenors, 24 basses, 16 to 20 altos, and 24 sopranos. However, different conductors exhibit a diversity of opinion on this point. It rather depends on what particular part or combination of parts should dominate the ensemble.

With a mass chorus, the balance is usually obtained by holding down the numerically stronger parts. Tenor sections may also be strengthened without harm to the ensemble by the addition of low altos.

Use of low altos

If the conductor wishes to have low altos sing the high tenor part along with a few (and sometimes very few) male tenors, he should caution the altos that all tones sung by them must be smooth and without edge. Even with an increase of power on loud chords, these altos must not be allowed to put an edge on the tone. If they will strive conscientiously to produce smoothness, which is approached at first by soft singing in the chest voice, no stridency will appear in the tenor part. Indeed, many such choruses do not show the slightest evidence of female tenors.

The unchanged boy voice

This presents the problem of the unchanged boy voice. Boys whose voices are not changed should preferably remain out of the chorus, particularly if there is evidence of effort or strain in their singing. If such a boy is put on the tenor part, he must be cautioned, as the altos have been, to keep the tone smooth and low. He must approach all power points easily and softly. Let the tenor effect come through quality rather than through quantity. Boys whose voices are of clear and velvety soprano quality may sing with the first sopranos. Any evidence that such a boy cannot sing high first soprano indicates that his voice is changing. It is not advisable to place him on alto parts. If he must sing at all, place him with the top tenors and let him sing an octave lower than he has been accustomed.

This produces two very good results. First, it helps to lower his voice, even quickening its descent. Second, it teaches him the idioms of the tenor part, which in all choral literature are different from the alto part. It is a certainty that he will eventually sing either tenor or bass. Therefore, when he once leaves soprano, he had best go at once to the tenor or bass part. It will do him no harm, whereas, to sing alto, is a waste of time and it may even serve to slow down his change of voice. In singing alto he may also acquire a guttural stridency which he cannot attain singing tenor. (It is physically impossible for him to sing such low tones loud enough to cause stridency.) On higher tenor tones he will receive the usual warning given to all altos and tenors singing the high tenor part, and all produce such tones easily. The boy must be watched and even changed to bass in a month's time, if his quality *thickens*. He may still be able to sing the tenor tones, but if his quality becomes thick and heavy, it is a sign that he is becoming a bass. He should be put on the bass part at once and his change of voice aided again in its descent. It appears that boys who leave boy soprano and go immediately to bass, are not harmed and often develop later into good *tenors!* On the other hand, placing a boy on tenor and keeping him there will mar the quality of his bass if he is developing in the bass direction and is placed there eventually.

General treatment

The general rule to follow is: Help the descent of the boy's voice by placing him on as low a part as is possible, even if he cannot sing all of the tones. The male voice will develop pure tenor more quickly if he goes down to the man's voice and then works up, even though it be from the depths of the bass. No strain is possible here and much physical development is actually aided by having him sing low.

No quarrel is intended here with those advocates of placing the boy down a step at a time until he attains his proper register. It is possible to have boy choruses of all four parts made up of boy singers exclusively, and they can do beautiful work. It is a question, however, whether these boys attain their natural voice tone as early as they should. The treatment of the boy voice should be to accelerate Nature's work rather than to gradually hold it back, even though the singing results in many boy choruses are admirable. It is a common observation that boy choirs are often pets of their conductors and that the actual vocal good of the boys is secondary to the conductor's desire to have a good choir!

Ranges

Quality being taken into consideration, the following is an approximate list of ranges of the various parts:

* 1st sopranos should vocalize † easily up to B-flat or C.
2nd sopranos should vocalize easily up to E-flat or F.
1st altos should vocalize easily up to C or D.
1st altos should vocalize easily down to middle C.
2nd altos should vocalize easily up to A or B.
2nd altos should vocalize easily down to A or G.

* 1st sopranos who can attain these heights are few, but their scarcity is a matter of no concern since a few of them can overbalance many times their number of lower voices. Girls who cannot attain this height are often placed in the 1st soprano part because of the unusual clarity and brilliance of the voice. They will be instructed that when approaching tones too high for them they are to leave them out. To allow them to strain at such high tones will flat the entire chorus. It will also undoubtedly do harm to the voice.

† By "vocalize" is meant singing on an open vowel such as "ah" or a focused vowel such as "oh".

1st tenors should vocalize easily up to G or A.

2nd tenors should vocalize easily up to E or F.

1st basses should vocalize easily up to D or E.

1st basses should vocalize easily down to G or F.

2nd basses should vocalize easily up to C or D.

2nd basses should vocalize easily down to D or C.‡

(No down range limit is given for sopranos and tenors. On account of the idioms of choral music, no bottom limit is necessary for these parts.)

‡ The writer has had many low bass boys who could make a musical tone on low E, and with a little training acquired the art of singing a low C before the season was over. This was in an ordinary public high school chorus.

CHAPTER VII

SEATING PLANS

There are many arrangements in use both for rehearsal and concert. Some which are the more practical are shown in the accompanying charts.

No. 1 Chart for a school chorus

This seating arrangement is effective with a choir of two hundred voices or more.

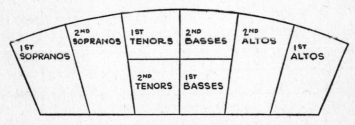

CHART No. 1

This plan is based on the raised platform arrangement. Here it will be noticed that the second basses and the first tenors are placed at a higher advantage than' their more powerful second tenor and first bass colleagues. The tone thus projects into a concert hall in proper relief, while the tone of the second tenors and the first basses is blanketed somewhat by being lower down and surrounded by the other parts.

The first sopranos and first altos, being the leading contrapuntal agencies, occupy the extremes. The answering figures which in many choral works are given to these two parts, are hurled back and forth with telling effect. The second sopranos and the second altos, who are used more frequently for the supporting harmony in conjunction with the middle choir of tenors and basses, are thus left intact and in close proximity to their most frequent collaborators.

The entire male section will keep on the pitch when enclosed on the two sides by the higher voices of the girls. *It is a mistake to put the boys' voices behind the girls. It causes much of the flatting that is so difficult at times.*

The third altos, that is, girls who sing the top tenor, should sit *back* of the boy first tenors. This will lend the boys strength and help them with the pitch. Even though these girls must sing softly, their presence and soft tones will lend confidence to the first tenor boys in front of them.

No. 2 Chart for school chorus

This chart is for a choir of any number up to two hundred voices seated on a raised platform.

In this case more overlapping of the parts is advocated, both to encircle the male voices and to allow for decreased numbers in such parts. In general, the same reasons apply to this arrangement as those given for chart No. 1.

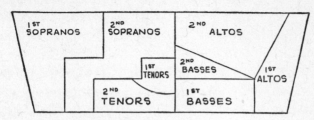

CHART No. 2

No. 3 Chart for school chorus

This chart is for a choir of any size that must stand on a level while singing.

CHART No. 3

The enveloping of the male section by the rest of the choir is still retained. A conspicuous difference is the placement of the first tenors beside the second tenors and the second basses with the first basses in regulation male quartet formation. This gives all four of the male parts access to the front line facing the audience. In the other charts this was effected by raising the first tenors and the second basses above the second tenors and first basses.

Any arrangement which places the male section behind the women's section, particularly on a level floor, will not give equally good results.

No. 4 Chart for professional choir

This arrangement is especially valuable when the choir remains seated throughout all numbers. A more complete discussion of this feature is to be found on page 133.

This chart is also based on the raised platform idea.

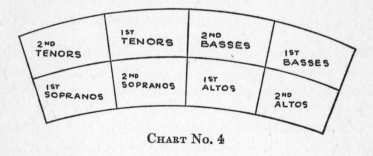

CHART No. 4

Double choir

It will be noticed that the men are behind the women but at this stage of advancement the male section does not depend on the women's section for pitch accuracy as it does in school choirs.

The peculiar arrangement of the male section is due to the ease with which double choir numbers may be sung without making any change in alignment. If the conductor wishes to have all the "firsts" sing the first choir part and all the "seconds" sing the second choir part, as is often the case, the choir is divided thus into two choirs each in contact with the other at the corners. A diagram of choir No. 1 would appear as follows:

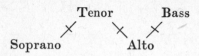

Choir No. 2 would appear as

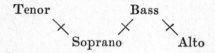

The whole choir is thus ready to sing numbers which call for re-enforced parts or for division into separate choirs. This may be effected without making it necessary for any member of the choir to change his seat.

If the conductor decides to have half of each part sing the first choir and second choir respectively, without division as to "first" and "second," he has only to draw his dividing line through the parts in the following way and his choir is still in contact at the corners:

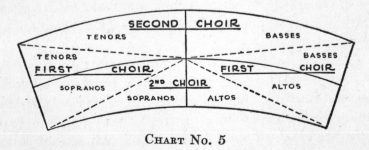

CHART No. 5

Having the double choirs in contact is vital to the smooth functioning of a double chorus. Such a division as the following would completely separate parts of each choir from others:

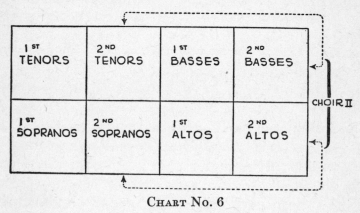

CHART No. 6

It will be noticed that here the two choirs interfere with each other. The only way to get them together without interference would be to have the singers change places on the platform.

CHAPTER VIII

FACTORS IN THE SUCCESSFUL FUNCTIONING OF A CHORUS

Officers

In school choirs it is advisable to have an election of officers as soon as the students have been together for a few weeks. By that time they will know whom they wish to select for the various offices. The conductor should pick his own nominating committee to canvass the field and to put up three good candidates for each office, except that of secretary and perhaps that of business manager. He should appoint these himself since they are his chief aids in matters of routine clerical work, running errands, arranging for concerts, stage settings, printing, publicity and various other activities of the same nature.

Part leaders

The conductor should appoint one superintendent of each part. It is the duty of these persons to look after the needs of their own sections and to report all absences to the secretary. For this reason, the conductor must appoint persons in whom he has confidence. Time should not be taken by the conductor for such routine matters as calling the roll. All such things must be made to function smoothly by the machine which the conductor creates, leaving to himself the task of teaching the music with a minimum of wasted time and energy.

Adult organization

In adult choir procedure it is well to form a board of directors, executive committee, and various sub-committees which will cause the choir to function without the conductor's personal attention. Aside from saving the conductor much worry, it creates a feeling in the minds of the members of the organization that they are managing their own choir and they are proud of it.

Distribution of music

When the choir is ready to begin rehearsals the music must be ready for them. The wise conductor plans his programs many months in advance and has all of the music ready or at a convenient place obtainable at a moment's notice. (See Page 123 on "Planning Programs".) This music should be distributed to the members once and for all time and should never be collected again! The members should pay for this music and learn to consider it as their own property. This saves time which is required to pass music about and gives the member a definite investment in the success of the organization. Such music may be taken home and rehearsed in much the same manner as other subjects may be studied at home. Copies which are lost or worn out are not likely, under this procedure, to cause any inconvenience to other members, which is often the case when the organization owns the copies and, after giving them hard usage, turns them in at the end of the season to what is practically a useless library. A very favorable attitude is thus created on the part of the member. He will take pride in building up his own library of good music which is his own property. This spirit should be fostered and encouraged because it means that in future years our people will view with just as much pride their private libraries of music as their libraries of acquired books.

In a public school even though music is purchased by the Board of Education and is issued for the use of students, it is best to arrange for each student to pay for his own copy in much the same manner as he provides his own pencils and other accessories. Thus the music will become the property of the student. Let the Board of Education money be spent in purchasing music for sight reading classes and for permanent additions to the school library of music. A good chorus should *read* through a hundred or so compositions a year without any attempt at memorizing for performance. Of course it would be financially impossible for most students to buy all of this music. Therefore let the school buy it and let the chorus member buy only that music which is worked on for concert purposes. He may then mark it to suit himself and make certain annotations which he may desire to refer to again at some future time, especially after he has graduated and has begun to accumulate a library of choral music which is his own.

In some schools a fee is set, subject to the approval of the parents, which covers the cost of all music used for the season. When the procedure of having the pupils pay for their own music is in doubt, it is well to have an announcement made to the candidates as they are "trying out." This announcement should state that each candidate is expected to purchase his own music and that an opinion from his parents is desirable. In most cases the students will have no difficulty in bringing from home the desired permission to purchase their own copies.

If a very obstinate case develops, which is rare, it would be best to have a friendly talk with the objector and to tell him that the music will be bought for him and that he may have it free of charge. The conductor can well afford to do this himself. It usually results in the student paying for it sooner or later, especially if the chorus has been a success and he has felt proud of his own membership in it. The purchase of music should not be made a *requirement* for entry without the parents' consent. With an adult choir it is, on the contrary, the only thing to do.

Type of music

The selection of music for the choir should depend on the program that has been planned. More on this subject will be found on page 123. It is well to include numbers of varying degrees of difficulty, so that the chorus may be introduced to an easier number and gradually brought to a higher state of proficiency as the season progresses. It is possible to obtain many such easy numbers which are in the class of standard works. In this manner the program will not have high class music mixed with music of mediocre rank. Many of the works of Lotti, Palestrina, Byrd, Purcell, Wilbye, and Bateson are excellent with which to start a choir rehearsing. Technically, these numbers do not present great demands, and yet, when learned they will maintain equal rank with the larger works which may come later. Consultation of the list of material on page 174 will furnish the conductor with many easy numbers with which to begin his work.

The proper "first" piece

Now and then it is the experience of a conductor that training a choir on a more difficult number at the outset will make it more proficient and faster moving when it is introduced to the remainder of the program. A case in mind is that of Bach's Motet, "Jesu Priceless Treasure". This work contains easy chorale verses and fairly difficult contrapuntal choruses. A choir that is started on this work will require a longer time to learn it, but will greatly benefit from the discipline necessary to perform it properly. Any numbers which the conductor may introduce to the choir after it has studied this number will seem much easier. At the same time, this motet contains enough color to interest even the most inexperienced, which cannot always be said of Bach's music.

Both methods of selection are to be advised, depending on the type of human material that confronts the conductor.

Capacity of a choir

It is not good practice to consider the *capacity* of a choir when selecting music. The conductor may plan his program and select the music long before he knows how many singers he will have or what will be their ability. Below the senior high school age, of course, this consideration must enter because of the limited range of the children. However, from senior high school on to adult choruses, the conductor must assume that these choirs will sing anything that he places before them. Physically and mentally they are able to do this. The voices are all there, the parts are all possible, even in the most difficult music. Therefore let the singers try their mettle without humoring them with consideration of their capacity. If the conductor concludes that a certain number would be ideal for the building of his program then, by all means, that number should be placed on the program and the choir taught to sing it even at the cost of great effort.

If, as occasionally happens, difficulties are encountered in matters of range, the conductor must use his own ingenuity in arranging a substitute for the tone which cannot be reached. This usually occurs only in very low bass. The tone an octave higher may be sung, as a rule, without affecting the aesthetic sense of the composition or destroying the tonal balance.

Underestimation

It appears that underestimation is one of the real obstacles to progress of American choral societies. The conductors themselves often entertain doubt as to a certain number and consequently hesitate to give it to the choir. The best procedure is to assume that the choir can sing anything and then proceed to attack and devour the number without saying anything to the choir about its difficulty.

Especially in high schools and colleges the young people have capacities for learning which are far in advance of what is usually thought possible. These young people are afraid of nothing and will sing anything if the conductor will approach the music in this fashion. Let us not be guilty of the timorous fault of underestimation of them. Youth loves to conquer!

Uniforms

Every choir should have a distinctive vestment. In the case of school choirs, these may be made from inexpensive material, using the school colors. Adult choirs have a choice of the regulation black choir vestment or one of their own design and color choice. These uniforms lend added distinction to the appearance of any choir and completely solve the problem of dress and its appearance to the audience. In many schools these vestments are made by the members of the chorus. A very simple plan for making them may be worked out which will seldom bring the total cost to a prohibitive figure.

Of course such vestments will not present the appearance of carefully tailored gowns, but as the choir sings en masse the effect on the audience is good and no defects are noticeable. In schools where these are made by members of the chorus, some plan may be worked out whereby the graduating members will leave their vestments as gifts to the chorus. In a few years the chorus will own enough so that there will be no necessity of making new ones.

The possession of vestments is not absolutely necessary. There are even times when vestments or uniforms are a distinct handicap! This occurs when the simplicity of the singers is displaced with an artificiality of mode and style. It would be far better to have a concert sung by people in their variegated clothing colors and types than in all the best and most stylish uniforms in the world, if on the one hand, they sang with spontaneity and simplicity of spirit, without pose and affectation, and if on the other hand they did not! The outward accoutrement can do harm as well as good and this point might be watched. Many choirs with beautiful vestments or uniforms assume an artificial pose, at a signal folding their hands or forearms into their robes across their stomachs with great aplomb, and proceed to sing with the precision and stance of puppets, eyes glued to a wildly waving director. It may be great "show-off" for someone, but it is not the song or the singing which is good, under such circumstances. The audience runs the gamut of emotion from amazement to ridicule and often considers the thing a sort of "stunt". Let the singing be natural and sincere and the stage deportment without affectation, vestment or no vestment.

Mental attitude of the choir

The place of the rehearsal, the time, the music to be sung, the division of parts, the possession of vestments and other factors all contribute to a proper general state of mind on the part of the chorus. Other things being equal, it is the duty of the conductor to place his singers in a receptive mood for that which he is about to give them. Many rehearsals go badly because the conductor himself is not in a good mood when he approaches his task.

Attitude of the conductor

The first precept is that the conductor must cultivate habits of thought which are designed to bring about patience, consideration for human faults and frailties, a sense of humor, an adaptability to unpleasant occurrences, fairness to all and a generally affable disposition. Strictness of method in handling disciplinary cases will then not be resented. Students are inclined to side with the conductor in controversies if, on the whole, he has been fair and honest in the display of the qualities enumerated.

CHAPTER IX

THE REHEARSAL

The conductor's exposition of the number to be sung

It will not suffice to call for rehearsal of a given number and begin immediately with a rehearsal of the parts. The conductor, who before this time has thoroughly familiarized himself with the number, will spend a few moments in forceful exposition of the piece. For example, in Bach's "Jesu Priceless Treasure", the conductor will point out the following things:

1. This number is based on an old chorale. Bach did not write this chorale. It was written by Johann Crüger about 1653. (The conductor will now play the chorale in full resonant piano chords, affecting the broad sweeping lines of a pipe organ rendition. He will then give a short explanaton of the nature of a chorale if he is asked as to its meaning. Otherwise he will wait until later. Too much talking right here may lose interest.)

2. Originally there were many verses to this old hymn, but Bach decided to use only four of them. After each verse Bach wrote in his conception of what each verse meant and its reaction on the singers. Immediately after the first verse Bach wrote his own chorus entitled "There is Now No Condemnation to Them Which are in Christ Jesus". This chorus is a carefully planned combination of hymn-chord style followed by a contrapuntal section.

(The conductor here demonstrates the two styles by playing just a bit of each.)

The second verse is slightly different from the first. (Conductor plays part of the second verse so that the students may hear for themselves.)

3. This is followed by Bach's trio for women, after which the mood changes and Bach now inserts one of his own choruses. ("Death I do not Fear Thee".)

4. The remainder of the verses are interspersed in the same manner with Bach's conception. (The chorus should be instructed to turn rapidly to the pages where these choruses are interspersed, noticing the hymn verses in between. These should not be played, since the discussion is now at a critical stage where more talking or playing may lose attention.)

5. Just for the pleasure of it the chorus will now sing each of the four verses. If mistakes are made, it does not matter. The soprano's carrying the tune can at least get through it to the end of the fourth verse, even though other parts may fall out and come in again. As soon as each verse is finished, the chorus will quickly turn pages to the next verse, skipping what is between. The last verse is the same as the first except for the words. (The chorus now tries this, making the best of it and deprecating their own blunders, but realizing how beautiful it is. This beauty is dependent on the way the conductor plays it, of course.)

6. When the choir has sung the four verses the conductor will remark "That was very good except for a 'few' mistakes". This will usually cause many smiles. It is now perhaps a good thing to learn one of the verses correctly. The third verse may be chosen as the one to start on. The rehearsal now progresses as with any number.

The conductor should not sit down while this demonstration is taking place, even when he goes to the piano to play the excerpts. He should play it, standing, facing his chorus. If the piano is not in such a position it should be moved so that it is, before the rehearsal begins.

No accompanist should be used. After repeated experiments with student and teacher accompanists it has been brought home with force that the conductor must hold the undivided interest and attention to himself. An accompanist, regardless of how excellent, cannot but act as a detraction from the main point. When the conductor himself is at the piano any immediate stop and start can be made very easily. He thus has control of the situation at all times and is not dependent on the human element of any other person.

This is just an example of how the conductor himself must take the center of attention and thoroughly "sell" the number to the singers.

Rehearsing the parts

After the number to be rehearsed has had its proper exposition, one part should be taken alone. At each rehearsal it is well to begin with different parts. The soprano part carrying the melody should be taken last, inasmuch as this does not give the other parts an opportunity to learn the tune and to perhaps sing it when they should be carrying their own part.

After two parts are learned up to a certain stopping point, it is well to put these two parts together and perhaps to go over them two or three times. A third part should then be taken alone and then with one of the two parts that have already been learned. Then take the three parts together. Finally add the melody part. This will bring out a few who insist on singing the melody an octave lower. Any mistakes in such parts should be recognized and the rehearsal stopped immediately. The part which has been the offender should be given another trial by itself.

It is not good practice to take more than a small section of a number at a time. Even to begin at the end and to go from there to the beginning, or to select a place in the middle of a piece will do no harm. Let sopranos and tenors sing together once, then altos and basses. Then varying it, let the sopranos and basses sing together while the altos and tenors do theirs following this. Progress to a new section of the composition should not be made until each part is perfect. This demands that the conductor shall have a good ear. Conductors who are unable to distinguish which part is singing wrong tones had better give it up as a bad job and go in search of some other occupation. Their choruses may sing passing well, but they will never produce outstanding results.

Individual corrections

It often happens that everyone on a part except perhaps one or two are singing correctly. The conductor, by this time able to leave the piano, must start one or two parts to singing and walk about among his singers, tapping gently on the shoulder any person whom he hears singing incorrectly. Often these singers will not be singing tones which produce dissonance or "discord." They are often heard singing some other tone in the same harmonic chord. This is commonly known as "faking." Kindly insistence on singing the correct tone, occasionally singing it with the person who is at fault, will usually correct this habit. The conductor must employ his own personality here on the side of creating a little amusement rather than a state of apprehension. It is far better to make a wry face at a boy who is growling a bass note of uncertain origin, bend over him and sing with him, stopping the choir on that particular chord and instructing them to hold the chord until he is through. He can then talk into the boy's ear and sing the right tone with him, perhaps slapping him on the shoulder or otherwise good-naturedly punching him. This will assuredly cause the other members to break into merriment occasionally but it will do no harm. Order can be restored by a few quick words or sharp raps of the baton on some nearby article.

Persistent off-pitch singers

One who persists in singing such wrong tones after repeated correction must be dealt with in some other fashion. His seat may be changed to one either beside or in front of a singer who sings rather aggressively and accurately. In many years of experience I have never known a case that would not eventually yield to this treatment and learn to sing the correct tones. Of course, if a person is totally tone deaf, that characteristic should have been discovered during his test for admission to the chorus, and he should not have been allowed to join the group in the first place. But these cases are rare.

If a person, during his admission test (see page 48), can sing the same tone as the piano sounds, both diatonically and by intervals, that is, by ascending the scale or by skipping around, he will respond to proper treatment in the chorus and will learn to sing correctly sooner or later.

Discipline

While one part is rehearsing it often happens that the other parts engage in conversation and much confusion. This is a result of laxity on the part of the conductor. It must not be allowed. Firmness but politeness will usually stop it. If the rehearsal of a part begins and another part begins to talk among themselves, stop immediately. It often is not necessary to say a word. The stop will focus attention on the reason. Begin again. If the talking begins again, stop immediately as before and look rather severely but not petulantly at the offenders. No word need be spoken as yet. If a third attempt is made and the talking begins again it is well to make a general statement to all that talking by anyone while another part is rehearsing will not be tolerated.

Right at this point is where many conductors lose control of their choirs. They make broad and sweeping statements to the whole class *before they begin* to rehearse, making dire threats as to what will happen to those who talk during rehearsal. Then, once the rehearsal is under way and an occasional talker is heard, nothing is done about it. Others about the talker soon learn that if they do not become too noisy the conductor will probably say little. This increases until the students are taking advantage of the conductor's silence on the point. Finally the teacher explodes with much vitriolic language and repeats the dire threat, even sending someone from the room.

Such unpleasantness can be avoided if the conductor will not allow the least bit of talking, from the beginning! It is best not to say anything about it until it occurs, and then follow the procedure advised in the foregoing paragraph. Any threats made are difficult to enforce, but once made they should be carried out. Displays of temper are to be avoided. If the conductor takes the more casual but firmer method, showing patience and a disposition to let the students correct themselves, little trouble will develop. And what is more valuable to him, he will secure the good will of the students and the general reputation of being a "good scout." Eventually these people will become very loyal to such a conductor and will go to almost any extreme for him. The teacher who announces in grand style what is going to happen to any offender and then allows it to drag along loses respect at the outset.

Occasional severity

Stern measures are now and then necessary. These should come so seldom that when they do they are positively startling. Oral chastisement should be cutting to the core and should be snapped with the precision of a football coach. This will startle the whole chorus into a state of paralytic indecision. The conductor should never rant nor dwell on his remarks. A few quick, well-ordered rebukes in a tone of voice that sounds dangerous will have the desired effect. Discipline is a problem which is usually made by the teacher himself. He must always be supreme but fair, strict and stern but sincere, assuming good order and not looking for trouble as the natural condition of things, an unmerciful driver of people to their tasks by remarks goading them to greater aggressiveness and enthusiasm but not to resentment.

Enthusiasm on the part of a conductor is a great boon. Placid people and those inclined to be unassertive will never become great conductors. Enthusiasm must abound to the point that people may often accuse the leader of being egotistical and conceited. But a magnetic leadership will usually become a contagion to alert students. It is impossible to please everyone. It is better to be on fire with enthusiasm for the work than to be worried about being considered conceited. Such opinion usually comes from those who cannot do the work they are criticizing. Jealousy plays a large part in such opinions.

Procedure with an adult choir is identical. Discipline is rarely a factor here. It is very bad procedure to speak to anyone by name in addressing remarks to an adult choir on matters of behavior or discipline. After the rehearsal, the offending party may be reported to the personnel committee or a personal talk may be had with him before so reporting him. In most cases, neither is necessary, for by the time of the next rehearsal, the offending party has either felt himself in a different state of mind or he has perceived the displeasure of others in the group at his own action. He usually corrects himself.

The human conductor

The conductor must always keep in mind that he is dealing with other human beings. They have the same idiosyncrasies and tendencies toward breaking over the bounds of behavior as he himself has. They, too, have their troubles and depressed states of mind. They, too, sometimes feel elated and sometimes physically and mentally below standard. A well-conducted rehearsal by a conductor with an understanding and sympathetic heart will often prove to clear up the atmosphere and send the singers home feeling much better than when they came.

CHAPTER X

TONE QUALITY

Exercises

Many systems of exercises are in use for the purpose of "warming up" the singers and putting them in shape for a rehearsal. Some of these do much good. It is a question, however, as to the relative advantage of such exercises compared with the working out of the same ideas on the actual piece of music being learned.

The average conductor is pressed for time. There is so much ground to be gone over in a given length of time! To take some of these precious moments for exercises which might be worked out in the composition seems rather a waste of time. Such matters as breathing, sight reading, tone quality, and intonation may indeed be much better worked out in an actual composition intended to be sung. It is preferable to go immediately into action with the rehearsal of the composition and to take up such projects or exercises as they present themselves. This method has come to be recognized as the most effective in such fields as piano playing, singing (solo), and general instrumental work. In the old days much attention was given to "technique" and volumes of exercises were published. The modern method is to solve technical problems and to develop proficiency in solving them directly from the music to be performed.

Sight reading exercises may be entirely dispensed with in modern choral works. Learning to sight read will come as a natural result of association of the singers with the numbers they are rehearsing. *There is then more reason for it!*

Tone quality exercises

It is well, during rehearsal, to make no mention of tone quality until the notes are fairly well memorized. Then a passage which is sung with bad tone quality may be taken alone. A very few words or perhaps a demonstration by the conductor of the kind of tone he desires and how to produce it will almost immediately elicit the result from the singers. If, upon singing the part again the quality is not improved, pause and demon-

---

FIGURE 1. The position of the head organs and cavities under average singing conditions: tongue depressed, oesophagus collapsed, mouth rounded, and passages into head cavities open. Reference to Figure 3 should be made constantly, since it gives the frontal view of this figure. It shows very clearly the interconnected cavities, while this figure (1) shows a division through the center of Figure 3, vertically.

Singers will be interested in the position of the turbinates—see both figures, 1 and 3—since these, when affected by a cold, become inflamed and enlarged, often closing the passage completely.

The nerves of smell-sense are extended into the region of these turbinates. They become cut off from the source of smell whenever a cold is experienced.

The sinuses should be noted, since they offer a source of great resonance to the singer's tone. At the same time, they must be carefully kept free from infection. When infected they fill, sometimes completely, and are extremely difficult to clear.

The sphenoidal sinus does not appear in Figure 3, since it is located between the frontal sinuses, but farther back, and is impossible to show in proper perspective.

strate again or speak a few words of encouragement. Urge that a more definite *mental* idea of this be maintained in approaching the tones. It may be necessary to make several trials.

Tone quality and the vowels

The accompanying diagrams illustrate the approximate relative position of each of the vowels as they are focused in singing. (See Figures 1, 2 and 3.)

Referring to Figure 2, following are a few salient features:

The focusing of these vowel sounds must not be confused with their placement. Experienced singers have learned to produce a tone focused naturally and to project it to a proper position or placement for the sake of good quality and resonance. Thus, "ah" can be sung with all the muscles at the base of the tongue relaxed, but it is placed for proper resonance, in the passages leading up into the head.

It is almost impossible to get good resonance and placement for the vowels "aw", "aa" (as in class) and "uh" (as in but). On the other hand, "oo" (as in moon) is naturally focused, in speaking, at or near the entrance to the head cavities and is easily placed. As progress is made toward the front of the mouth the distance from the back of the mouth is increased and projection is closer to nose and teeth, giving more pointed issuance to the sounds.

The most important vowel is "oh" which is located naturally in focus exactly in the center of the mouth cavity. It is a combination of all the vowels and offers an excellent medium for vocal exercise of tone quality, but not for flexibility, speed, resonance, or projection.

For speed and flexibility, "ah" is the best vowel because of the relaxed throat muscles.

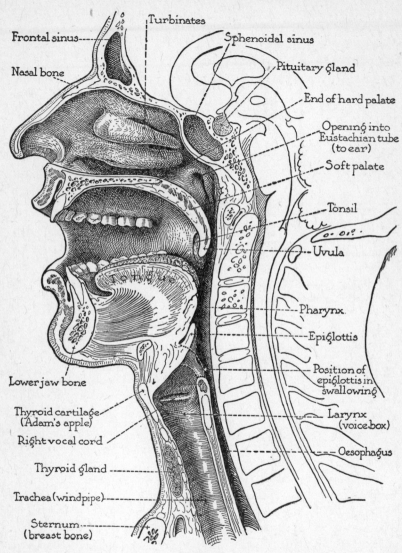

Frontal sinus

Nasal bone

Turbinates

Sphenoidal sinus

Pituitary gland

End of hard palate

Opening into
Eustachian tube
(to ear)

Soft palate

Tonsil

Uvula

Pharynx

Epiglottis

Position of
epiglottis in
swallowing

Larynx
(voice box)

Oesophagus

Lower jaw bone

Thyroid cartilage
(Adam's apple)

Right vocal cord

Thyroid gland

Trachea (windpipe)

Sternum
(breast bone)

FIGURE 1.

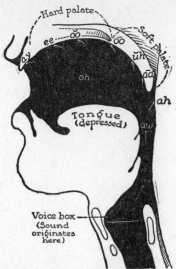

FIGURE 2. Showing approximate focal point for the vowels.

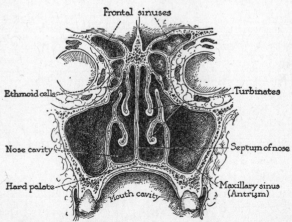

FIGURE 3. Frontal view of face and nasal cavities.

For resonance, "oo" (as in moon) is the best vowel to use in practice.

For projection of the tone outward and hence, clearness and precision, "ee" is the best.

All the other vowel sounds shown in the diagram are hybrids of "ah", "oo", and "ee", while "oh" is a combination of them all.

Choral tone

For the purpose of securing proper tone quality a chorus should be interrupted now and then in its rehearsal, whenever the vowel "oh" presents itself. Each part should hold this vowel, making sure that the mouth is rounded and that pure "oh" is issuing. Unless definite mental thought is given to this the singers, without being conscious of it, will often sing "uh" (as in but) producing a sound which resembles a prolonged grunt.

A simple chord should then be given to each part, such as

and the chorus instructed to hold this chord for different lengths of time. The chorus should practice crescendos and diminuendos while holding this "oh" tone; also attack sharply and smoothly, quickly and slowly, release in the same manner; then dynamics from fortissimo to pianissimo.

The chorus is then moved up, each part a half-step, and the performance repeated. Again rise a half-step, continuing in this fashion until the range top is not far away. Repeat in descending order as many times as advisable.

Let the women practice their part of the chord alone while the men listen, and then let the men practice while the women listen. With urging and encouragement, the tone will improve each time until the chorus members who are listening will show by facial expression that they are enjoying the beautiful sounds.

The composition should now be referred to once more and the spot where the tone quality was deficient should be sung again. It will usually improve not only that particular spot, but the territory on both sides of the spot.

When tone quality is objectionable on other vowel sounds, repeat the "oh" exercise and instruct the chorus to sing the different vowels with the "feeling" that they are singing "oh". This will destroy pronunciation at first, but will develop a definite mental approach to all vowels in the matter of tone quality. Clarity of pronunciation will resume its natural trend, but there will be a "carry-over" of the "oh" quality.

To develop resonance

While the holding of long tones and chords on the vowel "oh" will introduce a certain amount of resonance, the main value of the "oh" is in its round and velvety smoothness which can develop into sonority without attaining hardness when under strong pressure. Singers who are accustomed to throaty conversation will need corrections on the matter of throwing the tone into the head and away from the back of the tongue.

For this purpose "oo" (as in moon) is ideal. Whether the tones be sung piano or forte is immaterial. The tones will roll through all the passages of the head with great resonance. This will *not* increase good tone quality in and of itself. The custom which is in use in many schools, of having children vocalize entirely on this vowel is likely to lead to effortless, lifeless tone, lacking volume and quality. But it is an invaluable vowel for the purpose of throwing the tone away from the hard focus.

Here again the singing of a part which has particularly blatant lines can be aided by singing it with the same feeling as is produced when singing "oo". Chords and parts of the same composition may be sung entirely on "oo". It is not at all objectionable to sing an entire number, if it is short, on the vowel "oo".

To develop projection

Resonance and quality are valueless without a definite feeling of placing the tone as far forward as possible: The "ee" vowel gives the sensation of being thrown out by the teeth, and the singers should be rehearsed now and then on getting the mental feeling of actually projecting this vowel to a point *in front of the teeth.* Not much of this should be done as it will produce tight throats and bad tone quality. It has the same effect as constant humming. In fact, humming, unless it be without pressure and high in the head, will place the tone in almost the same spot behind the teeth as does the vowel "ee".

Humming

This fad has become almost a vocal monstrosity. It was originally introduced by composers to form a rather string-like effect as an accompaniment for a solo voice or for some especial effect to be gained from the text. Because of its novelty conductors everywhere have taken it up until it is not unusual to hear a chorus rehearsal begin by humming a number and then singing it using the words. This humming has no qualities that will *improve* tone quality and should be avoided except when used deliberately to secure a definite effect of instruments or other weird and unvocal effects. It is very valuable to the a cappella choirmaster for just this sake alone, but a good choirmaster should never use this as a warming process or for tone improvement. It would be far better to use the vowel "oo" or "oh" for warming up, depending on whether resonance or smoothness is desired.

To develop flexibility and speed

For many centuries the best vowel for this purpose has been the "ah" vowel and it remains so today. The muscles at the base of the tongue must be relaxed if this vowel is used long. Exercises based on a number being rehearsed are plentiful for the employment of "ah". Bach's cantatas are full of coloratura passages. An easier number, suitable for beginning chorus, is "Oh Saviour Burst the Heavenly Bound" by Brahms (Musical Research Society edition). On the last two pages of this number occur some of the best passages for practice of "ah" by a school or adult chorus. These passages, incidentally, are set to the first syllable of the word "Amen", showing Brahms' own idea of its adaptability. The vowel "ah" is not especially good for the practice of good tone production, since it opens the throat.

Each of the vowels encountered in choral music has its own particular use. It is rather difficult to use any one of them to suit the functions of all, unless it be "oh", which is the nearest approach to them all combined. For tone quality alone, nothing can surpass this euphonious little vowel which after all sounds so big.

CHAPTER XI

INTONATION

On this point choral conductors rise or fall. Let all choirs learn as perfectly as they may to sing every note that was ever written and then fall short in matters of staying on the pitch and the story of complete dissatisfaction has been written. Nothing destroys the morale of a chorus in concert like untrue intonation. A flatting group will often become completely demoralized and the audience, whether conscious of it or not, will certainly not feel edified.

How can good and perfect intonation be attained for a chorus of human beings? And how can it be made perfect under any condition of temperature or temperament? Many choral conductors would give a fortune to know the answer to this. It is evident that there is no answer or it would have been discovered long ago!

However, there are certain phases of a conductor's work which entail much experiment on this point. It is entirely possible for a chorus to attain such perfection in matters of pitch that they *very rarely* flatten, and then only when some unlooked for and unusual factor is encountered at the moment.

Causes of poor intonation

Perhaps the discovery of a remedy for bad intonation would lie first in a consideration of the causes of it. The main causes which have come under my observation and experiment are:

1. Bad tone quality and production.
2. Lack of mental alertness.
3. The worn musical groove.
4. Extreme heat.
5. Absorption of tones by surroundings.
6. Physical fatigue.
7. Defective hearing.

In the past twenty years it has been my custom to eliminate these *causes* until I think I am justified in saying that not one of my choirs, singing in concert, reviewed by a critic of the first class, has yet been said to have flatted. It has required constant and unceasing watchfulness. Habit is a powerful thing. Choruses which form a habit of flatting will with difficulty overcome it. The conductor must therefore not allow, even for an instant, the slightest flatting. This demands that he himself have a good ear. Ability to detect the flatting even of a few vibrations can be acquired by application to the task of listening, of comparing tones, of thinking higher, of making it a definite point to be extraordinarily particular. Much of flatting is perhaps due to plain mental relapse. The conductor must be so eager to catch it and stop it immediately that he will even anticipate it. There are certain places in all music where flat-

ting is more likely to occur. The conductor shall anticipate the following opportunities:

1. Ascending melodies will be observed to reach the top of
   the musical hill a little under the pitch with the average
   unaccompanied singer.
2. Intervals which leap from the medium part of the voice
   into the top part must be watched *at the top*.
3. Melodies which descend and then turn upward again to
   resolve will generally offer a place for the resolution to
   be slightly under the pitch.
4. Recurring intervals in sequence, such as two or three
   fourths in succession, will rarely come out on the same
   tone as the one with which they started.
5. Leading tones, especially on inner parts, are very likely
   places for flatting to occur. The tenor and alto parts
   especially should be watched.
6. The occurrence of a sharped fourth after a natural
   fourth in a modulation (which is the same as a leading
   tone) will usually give cause for attention.
7. Sustained tones of any considerable length may sag even
   while the singer is holding. This is due to lack of breath
   control. (See Breathing, Page 100.) ,

These are only a few of the places which the conductor must anticipate and be forewarned against in choral
music. Let us take up a discussion of each of the reasons
given for bad intonation and suggest ways and means of
combating them.

1. *Bad tone quality and production.* Singing from the
   throat without proper focus and resonance will not give
   the singer a "sense" of his own flatting. His own ears
   will not hear because his own tone is not brought into
   direct contact with them in resonance. To overcome this

defect, practice the methods already discussed for attaining good tone quality and proper placement.

2. *Lack of mental alertness.* The singers will often in the course of a rehearsal lapse into a more or less relaxed mental condition. There is no immediate need for excitement or for especial verve. Especially is this true if the singers know their notes and have memorized the piece. The very fact that they do know it so well will put them off guard. They forget to think constantly about the next tone they are going to sing. To combat this, the singers must be constantly kept alert; they must be told to think always of what they are singing and not to sing absent-mindedly. It must be incessantly drilled into them to "think high". The approach to a tone can just as well be from on top of it rather than from below. All singers when approaching a higher tone should be told to imagine that they are coming to that tone from above it rather than reaching up to it! Added to this is the injunction that while they are imagining that they are higher, their tone quality must be good. It is possible (I have done it many times with choirs) to have a chorus sing a number all the way through and raise it in pitch from one to three half-steps while singing it, merely by thinking deliberately that they are going to do it.

Caution should be exercised here. Singers will not sing higher by exerting more power! It is often the case that a conductor signals for a higher pitch as the group is singing. They immediately push harder to get that tone. This must be warned against and the chorus made to get the higher tone by *mental* effort, even though they approach it pianissimo. This pushing harder to go higher will not only not secure a good tone on the pitch, but will generally result in just the opposite effect from what the conductor tried to get. It will usually result in flatting, rather than the correction of flatting.

3. *The worn musical groove.* This is a most pernicious and undermining influence to flatting. The chorus sings the number in the same key every day, or at every rehearsal, until it becomes accustomed to a certain pitch. Constant repetition of this pitch creates a "groove" which tends to wear ragged with constant use. There are perhaps no physical reasons for dropping out of this groove; the reasons are probably psychological. That is to say, the mental alertness and general spirit of the singers decline because of the sameness of tone with each rendition. Each repetition tends to produce monotony. This quality destroys spontaneity and causes a dropping of energy and spirit.

To combat this, it is well to sing the number in different keys. The singers do not necessarily have to be informed of this; they will find it out for themselves by a realization of the newness with which the song seems to have become imbued. In the method I have developed for giving the singers their pitch in concert, the singers do not know in what key they are going to sing the numbers until they are ready to go onto the stage. Even then I may, during a concert, signal for a different key for the next number.

4. *Extreme heat.* The conductor should pitch numbers higher when in an extremely warm room. Since warm air is not as good a conductor of sound waves as is cold air, the singers will find themselves exerting more energy to project their tones. Added to the fact that warm air is enervating to the body, this quickly produces a fatigue, resulting in lowering of pitch.

5. *Absorption of tones.* Absorbing walls, curtains, and draperies will deaden the sound of the ensemble to such an extent that the resonance of the group is reduced to a minimum. No reinforcement from the harmonic relationship is felt and a lowering of the pitch is apt to take

place. Radio studios are usually unsatisfactory places for choral singing unless they have means of brightening the walls, causing more reflection of tone-waves. Concerts held on stages of acoustically good theaters may turn into flatting affairs because the tones are absorbed by the back-stage hangings or the space over the stage. Conductors should contrive some sort of sound board or reflecting device to be placed over the heads of the singers when singing in such places.

6. *Physical fatigue.* Physical, as well as mental fatigue, causes much flatting, especially in concerts. The conductor should do all in his power to keep his choir in a rested condition. Long tours have a wearing effect. A choir which remains seated while singing will be saved much of this fatigue. It is possible to do this and yet sing just as perfectly as when standing. This is further discussed in the chapter on "Concerts", page 133.

7. *Defective hearing.* Now and then certain singers who do not show any signs of defective hearing will gain admission to a chorus. These can be corrected by the conductor's insistence on their change of mental attitude toward the tones they are singing.

Psychology of the process

During the rehearsal on tone quality and intonation it is often advisable to adopt metaphorical expressions regarding certain kinds of tonal effects that the conductor wishes to bring out. It does not suffice merely to tell the choir to get a good tone. It may be that the use of expressions such as the following may bring about results more quickly. There are such contrasting expressions as:

Soft tone or *hard* tone
Light tone or *heavy* tone
Serious or *gay*
Dark or *bright*
Warm or *cold*
Colorful or *plain*
Happy or *sad*
Wild or *reverential*

Such a transference of thought, from the actual mechanics of tone placement and focus, to the mental idea to be sought, will often result in securing the result more quickly.

CHAPTER XII

INTERPRETATION

Tempo

The tempo of the composition being rehearsed is to be given correctly to the chorus at the very outset. This may be done during the conductor's exposition of the number. It is psychologically incorrect to begin rehearsal on a number at very slow speed and then work up to the proper tempo, unless the chorus has first heard it the way it should go. Regardless of how accelerated is the movement, the chorus should bear it at its full speed and with the possibilities of climax in mind, in order to gain an impression of that for which they are striving. The average number sounds very uninteresting when taken at a snail-pace and no interest on the part of the chorus is stimulated by such an introduction to it.

For purpose of diversion and perhaps amusement, it is often well, after the chorus has learned one section of a new number, to take the number up to proper speed, regardless of how fast it may go. This will occasion much excitement during the effort to stay with the part that each has learned. It is somewhat like a game in its appeal. Even though mistakes, at this speed, are made it will serve to make the singers more careful of the dangerous curves in the number when they go over them slowly, for they will realize that when that number is sung in tempo there will be certain spots for which they must be on the look-out.

Other factors

Interpretation partakes of the following: Dynamics, attack and release, breathing, ensemble, mood, eloquence, pronunciation, inflection and appearance. Interpretation should be taught when the number is memorized or very nearly memorized, so that the singers may give their undivided attention to the conductor.

Dynamics

The conductor proceeds to the explanation of the crescendo and diminuendo. He gives the chorus a convenient chord to hold using the vowel "oh". The baton, held with the point low, is pianissimo. As the conductor raises the "stick" very gradually the tone must increase until the full height is reached. The conductor, during this demonstration, must appear to grasp the baton more tightly and powerfully as he "pulls" up, exhibiting the greatest apparent force when he holds the stick point high in the air. (The arm should be slightly curved or bent at the elbow, not straight out.) The reverse order is then demonstrated down to the most pianissimo "fade-out".

This is very good discipline for the singers since it will teach them to graduate their tones so that they will not get too loud before the conductor reaches the full height, and conversely, that they are not to let the tone die until he has reached the extreme bottom again. These long crescendos and diminuendos may take thirty seconds or longer and should be dwelt on for five or ten minutes.

Attack and release

To drill for attack and release, let the chorus sing any convenient chord again using the vowel "oh" and attacking the chord sharply with each new signal of the baton. Release of each chord must occur at the exact split-second.

(1) The conductor should practice a definite sharp attack, hold and crescendo to sharp release.

(2) Then attack fortissimo and diminuendo to soft but exact release.

(3) Then attack softly but with precision, swell out and back and release softly.

(4) Attack softly but rather smoothly and slowly as if carefully sailing onto the tone, as contrasted with hitting it sharply. Variations of these forms and combinations with dynamics will give great variety.

(5) The conductor will now practice a series of quick short attacks. He will "throw" the baton at the chorus for just a fraction of a second and release immediately. Some singers will be heard hanging on. Repeated trials with this instantaneous attack and release are very valuable for precision.

(6) These short attacks then should be done in varying series. One, then three or four in quick succession, then other groups in quick succession.

(7) Then they should be done with varied *spacing between* the attacks.

(8) Finally without warning he should not release the attack as he has been doing, but hold the stick in the air for the choir to remain singing. Very few of the choir will hold on the first time because they have been accustomed to expect a quick release as well as a sharp attack.

(9) The conductor should then attack and hold one or two different length tones ending with a series of "shorts", repeating as though singing a telegraphic code. This exercise will do more than anything else to improve the alertness of the singers, because they never know what the conductor is going to do.

Breathing

The conductor, in explaining breathing, should state that all choral tones are held indefinitely, according to his wishes, and not because the music says they should be held any definite number of beats. What the individual singer cannot do, the choral body can.

The chorus is given a tone on vowel "oh" and instructed to hold it. The average newcomer will try to hold onto the tone until his lungs collapse. He will usually precede this by filling the lungs to the utmost capacity. This will cause a wavering tone, since the breath flow through the vocal cords cannot be controlled for any extended period under all conditions of holding. The lungs in such a case will eventually clamor for a release of the surplus air that is being held and may even cause the singer to involuntarily expel what is left in the lungs in one grand collapse.

The *normal breath* must be taken and control established. Then the tone will be held until the first sign of weakness appears. The singer will then take another normal breath and come back in on the tone which is still being held by the other singers. *No two singers will take a breath in precisely the same place.* The result is that the chorus, individually, is constantly being supplied with fresh normal breaths and the control of the tone is thus kept in hand. To an audience the appearance is of a choir holding a chord to unheard-of lengths.

The conductor may hold the chord for five minutes just to demonstrate that the chorus could go on singing and holding the same chord indefinitely. This fascinates the singers and inspires them with confidence.

This drill is very valuable in singing series of chords or melodic passages which call for very long and sustained holding. The singers will not attempt, in many cases, to hold the chords or phrase over to its logical end but will take several individual breaths before that point is reached. However, when the point of punctuation is reached, the whole chorus appears to have stopped at the same instant, after prolonged holding.

Breathing must occur (so far as the *chorus* as distinguished from its individuals is concerned) at natural places of punctuation, in the same manner as if the text were being spoken. No chorus breath should be taken in the middle of a sentence or natural clause, especially between the verb and its object. Individuals of the chorus may take breaths at any time providing they come back in immediately and without noticeable increase on tone.

Where the number of singers is smaller, the breath must be taken (during the chorus breath) much oftener than with a group of *many* individuals. These more frequent breaths keep the tone more constant. Otherwise the taking of individual breaths may be noticeable when they come back in on the tone again.

Breathing exercises

Apart from music in the actual singing, there is a feeling on the part of many that some sort of breathing exercises should be engaged in at the outset of a rehearsal. The proper use of the diaphragm in breathing and the correct posture can thus be demonstrated either standing or sitting. However, the same holds true as for matters of vocal exercise books, as discussed at the beginning of Chapter X. If the time of rehearsal is short and there is much ground to be gone over, it would be better to dispense with formal exercises in breathing at the beginning of each period and to take it up as part of the music being learned. The same fundamental things can be illustrated and incorporated into the actual learning of a number. In the last analysis, local conditions will largely govern and the teacher will have to decide for himself. If there is time for it and if the attention of the class can be held, well and good.

Memorization

Since the subject of memorization of music has often been made a part of the general subject of "interpretation", perhaps it should be discussed briefly here. As a matter of fact the factors in interpretation do not admit of qualification as to whether or not the notes of a composition are memorized! The factors governing interpretation are those which have to do with the proper conveyance of the composer's ideas to the listening audience. Memorizing may or may not improve the composition. Let us examine this statement for a moment.

It might be assumed that because a chorus, or any other sort of performing unit, had memorized the notes or words, or both, of a composition, it would be in a better position to watch the conductor, to sing as one unit and to more expertly express itself. This assumption would be correct only under certain conditions. One of these would be that all singers had memorized the number equally well. If some of the singers or players knew the number well and the remainder "leaned" on those who thus knew the work, the situation would be that of certain leaders being sure of what they were doing and certain others only following these leaders. Certainly this could not make for precision or sureness in attack, or in any other detailed point. This actually happens in case after case of performing units, especially under stress or stage fright.

Another phase of the memorization idea is that, although the performing unit were perfectly at ease and all able to get through the work without fright or lapse of memory, the perfection of ensemble caused by watching the conductor and understanding him so perfectly might cause quite an extended degree of mechanical precision! Many choirs have the precision and mechanical perfection of a highly adjusted machine, yet their singing leaves the audience more amazed by the mechanical aspects of the case, than moved by the message of the song. It would be far better in such cases for the humanness of devotion to ideas and their expression to be apparent in relaxed demeanor and poise. The day is past when the American public should be fed with sensationalism even in the memorized stunts of a performing group.

What does all this mean? Should memorizing be abandoned in favor of the printed music in the hands or on the music racks? Perhaps a medium position might be found which would be more to the point. The question is: Is this music memorized *as an end in itself,* or for the betterment of the song? Is memorization to be put up as a *requirement* for good singing, or is it going to be allowed to develop naturally so that by the time the number is learned the singers will almost sing it by memory, of their own free will and accord? This latter method of approach, at least psychologically, should, by all that is fair in argument, bring about a real state of singing the true meaning of the song. For if one knows and loves a song and its text so well that it just pours

out naturally and becomes a part of the singer's own
emotional experience, then, and only then, will the
singer become an actor living his part. Then, and only
then, will he "forget himself" and his appearance and
make the audience also forget him. Memorization in
such a case would indeed be ideal.

Is it not also possible to have this same learning and
living of the number with the printed score in front of
the performer? Is it not even an advantage at times
to have such a score for reference? Would it not at least
be conducive to less nervousness, and thus set up an
atmosphere of finished and deliberate artistry? The
great symphony orchestras of the world very seldom
play numbers from memory and yet the members of
such organizations really *know* what is coming next in
the score, and how it should be interpreted. The reaction
of the individual players in such an organization is often
actually sympathetic in telepathic response to the conductor because these players have a constant reference
before them as to what is going to happen next, and
they "feel along" with the conductor in spirit. And, as
for the artistic part of it, is there not a lost art in some
quarters, particularly choral—namely, the lost art of
intelligent score reading? Choirs all too often learn a
number by memory, concentrating on notes which are
often given them by rote, or by following a piano or
other means of "pounding out" the part, without having
the least idea of how to read and feel the music as they
go along, noting what is coming in the next bar or so
and preparing themselves for it.

Memorization which is put up as a requirement, as a "must", so to speak, usually curtails the sight reading ability of singers. Singers are notoriously poorer sight readers than instrumentalists. One reason is, that even in the schools, the boys and girls in the bands and orchestras are playing through, reading through, if you please, pages and pages of music without any intention of memorizing it. They learn to follow the page and the line of notes. They learn to read by position. Singers do not have this advantage. Even from early grades they have in many instances depended on rote learning and memorization! However, in certain places, repertoire reading classes in choral music are being set up. The purpose of these classes is to read through a hundred or more choral compositions per year without attempting to memorize or prepare for performance. Students who attend these classes, which in some cases are made a requirement by the choral director before admittance to the choral groups of the school such students invariably are better sight readers. There is no question but that the ineptitude of singers in reading is due to this lack of familiarity with scores. It would be far better to dispense with memorization entirely if a choice had to be made between memorization for its own sake and general musicianship!

One other feature usually advanced is that singers look badly holding music in their hands. Perhaps many of them do, but there is no reason why they cannot be made to look well, in fact *more* business-like and efficient with music in their hands than folded like mummies into some sort of robe and singing like robots. The only vital reason which can be thought of, when it comes right down to honest admission about this,—the only real reason for dispensing with music in the hands is when a part is to be acted in an opera, when the hands are not to be hampered with an object to carry about. Otherwise, why insist that it be left off stage? After all, the audience knows that there is or was some printed music somewhere once upon a time from which the chorus learned these notes. What shame is there in bringing the precious stuff in and letting the audience see an intelligent reading of it? As for watching the conductor while holding music in the hands, here again is a lost art among choral people, an art which instrumentalists mastered long ago.

Summarizing as to memorization: Where the memorizing process comes naturally with the performer and is not made a requirement or an end in itself, it is advisable and, in fact, praiseworthy. Where it hampers sight reading, reading of scores, general musicianship, and tends to create artificial and stunt performances, it is not to be recommended.

Ensemble

The exact split-second singing together of many individuals calls for perfect attention both with eye and mind. It is not necessary that music be memorized in order to secure this perfection. Such a feeling for singing together is more psychic than it is physical. Rhythm and harmonic modulatory sensations play a large part, to be sure, but more important is intelligence as to score and feeling for the music. Lack of these latter qualities will become apparent at once when approaching a broad ritard or other point of pause. Whether memorized or not, the music will be sung as a unit only if it is *felt* as a unit.

Mechanically the chorus can do much by using ordinary alertness of eye and ear. Many singers think they are singing strictly with the beat when in truth they are a matter of a fractional second behind the beat. Others perhaps sitting beside them are exactly with the beat. This, although not noticeable to any marked degree, brings about an effect of sluggishness. When every singer sings exactly at the same precise moment with the indication of the conductor, then and only then will the effect be one of perfect ensemble.

Mood

Learning must be with the spirit of the text in mind as well as of mere fixation of habit. The words of the text must be understood and their mood expressed. Therefore, choruses, if they memorize the words, must memorize the mood and do their utmost to express this in earnestness of voice and facial expression. A chorus otherwise will have mechanical perfection but be lacking in a deeper emotional value.

Eloquence

Eloquence depends on the mood established. The chorus which delivers the phrase with the greatest

amount of eloquence is that one which feels the emotion
or expression called for by the text and transfers it to
the listener by means of the greatest stress or lack of
stress on the text. For example, in the opening bars of
Tschaikowsky's "O Blest Are They," (Musical Research Society edition) the women's section is offered an
opportunity on the very first word. "O" should begin
with velvety smooth, round "oh" vowel, perfectly balanced as to parts. Before going on to the next beat, as
called for strictly by the marked tempo, the conductor
will cause the sopranos and altos to make the slightest
crescendo while clinging to the "O" and then push this
sound over into the word "Blest", stressing the word
with pressure. The remainder of the phrase, "are they,"
seems to emanate from the word "Blest" and is not to
be accented or stressed.

The first tenors, who now enter, do not linger on the
"O" but proceed immediately to the word "Blest". At
this precise instant the women's voices release, leaving
the tenors suspended alone for just a moment. Here the
thought is transferred from the chordal effect of the
women's part to a purely fine-spun tone of transparent
beauty on the part of the first tenors. But before the
attention is allowed to remain on this part the other
men's parts are brought in as if answering the first
tenors. This is repeated in entirety by another chord of
the women stressing "O" and "Blest," followed by first
tenor floating alone and answered by the other men. To
sing the number exactly as written without the stressing
and lingering on the parts as described gives much

beauty but lacks in spirit. The chorus singing in any other fashion does not seem to be "in earnest."

Before the men have released the last tones the sopranos begin a new musical idea with the word "raptured" followed in by the other parts and coming to rest in a simple reverential chord on the word "thrice-fold." The "oh" vowel in "fold" offers an excellent opportunity to blend the parts in a tone of great beauty and at the same time gives an impression of great profundity without singing loudly.

The basses now take up a steady climb to the first climax which occurs with the "Blest are they now and forever." This phrase should be slightly broadened and the utmost in tone pulled out without verging on the fortissimo. There is then a moment of absolute silence, after which the entire four parts sing, as if an after thought, "Let them rest in peace." Tschaikowsky has a dotted eighth note on the word "rest." The conductor will hold this slightly longer before he proceeds to the words "in peace," which are to be sung without the slightest accent. During this hold the altos who have a dissonance against the soprano, pull out the tone of their part slightly against the tone of the soprano, giving an effect of pathos and perhaps longing or earnest desire.

Immediately on the release of "peace" the women should be brought into another chord on "O" in the same fashion as at the beginning. This is now a recurrence of the first thought and should express more gloriousness than before, at the same time quickening the tempo slightly, thus giving an expression or reiteration,

without monotony, of the first thought but with rapid
progress to the second thought which is "Now rest
they ever in celestial home." In this phrase the altos proceed downward as if to finality and even pull their tone
into stress against the sopranos in the "lest" syllable
of "celestial." The chorus should hold this syllable
while the altos are pushing theirs into view. The "ial"
syllable is passed over quickly and without accent, coming to rest and a feeling of great blessedness on the
word "home."

The whole chorus now galvanizes into vigor and action with the words "Let their remembrance be forever"
and continues up to the main climax of the composition
on the words "to all nations." On the word "nations"
care should be taken not to allow the chorus to accent
the "tions" syllable more than the "na" syllable.

A long and dramatic pause occurs after this fortissimo chord. Then reverently the sopranos and altos
begin the closing "alleluia's" followed in by the men
and working into a pseudo-polyphonic entrance of each
succeeding part and building up in waves to a final but
secondary dynamic climax and then rolling, as it were,
down the shores of Time to a point of pause just before
the last three "alleluia's."

These last three are entered with great profundity
and with receding tone, slightly stressing the "lu" syllable and completely smothering the "ia" syllable. Even
though pianissimo, this gives the listener a feeling of
great intensity of thought.

This display of eloquence is possible with a minimum

amount of rubato. In fact, no rubato is noticeable if the proper eloquence and expression is used, since the delivery of the text has been logical and normal. Any slight acceleration of the tempo or subsequent ritard has been with regard to the emphasis placed on the text and has not been done for undue display or false dramatic show. The number may then be said to have been sung with eloquence.

Inflection

Inflection is a result of eloquence. The mode first being established and the feeling given out eloquently, the proper inflection must be extended to the words.

It is possible to have diction without eloquence but it is impossible to have eloquence without good diction. Thus the pronunciation of words may be clear and distinct, the proper syllable may be stressed, and the unaccented syllable tempered, and yet the mood of the number will not have found its way through the text to the ears of the listener.

Inflection is described in such passages as "Now rest they ever" in the composition just mentioned. The first three words are about equally stressed and smoothly passed over. On the word "ever" the majority of choruses will lightly stress the syllable "ev" and land rather heavily on the syllable "er." The order must be reversed and the "er" should change to "uh" with the slighter "r" given on the release of the word.

Another example is the following phrase which is quite common in many compositions: "We will praise

Thee, O God." Without thinking, the average chorus will run the "Thee" and the "O" together, making the smoothly flowing word combination, "Theeo". Good inflection will stress the word "praise" so that "Thee" may be pronounced back in the mouth and cut off quickly and without accent. The "O God" will then come after the smallest interval of *complete silence* on the part of every singer.

The habit of running words together is perhaps one of the most difficult to eliminate. "O Blest Are They" is usually sung "O Bless Star They"; "Guide us on our way" is usually sung "Guy duh sah nour way". *Practically every line* of a song has these elisions which will come to the fore in singing more prominently than in speaking. The teacher should study these lines, *anticipating every possible place* where this can happen, and then drill the chorus in correct separation of the words. This proper separation, combined with good inflection and clear diction will result in almost complete clarity of text, so that any audience will be able to understand clearly. Proof of this is to be found in abundance when a chorus sings by radio. Here the mouths of the singers cannot be seen. What comes out of the loud speaker is a run-together jumbled group of unintelligible syllables which will become intelligent enough when properly put in focus. A general rule to follow is to sing as one would properly speak. In this connection it might be well for all choral teachers to take a course in Speech so that they might become conscious themselves of these glaring word monstrosities which choirs will just naturally sing.

Word. pronunciation

Individual word pronunciation is based on a combination of vowels and consonants. The vowels are for the producing of tone and the consonants are for the start and release of the tone. For this reason the vowels should be studied and the mouth kept open and the tone placed with due respect to the particular vowel being used until it is time to "release" or stop the word and go on to the next word. Here the consonant forms the closing of one word and the beginning of another one.

Pure vowels, in singing, are "Ah", "Oh", "Oo" (as in moon) and "Ee". Variations of these may be found in all shades. "Ah" has its family, beginning with "aw" at the bottom of the throat, and ending with a shallow "aa" (as in hat). "Uh" is really a variant of "Oh"; "Eh" is a variant of "ee", being merely back farther from the teeth with the mouth more open, and so on. The sound of the English long "A", as in "day", (Latin long "E") is really a combination of a broad "Eh" and "Ee" with a lingering on the "Eh" and a slight release, be it ever so slight, by the use of "Ee". In fact it is impossible to say this sound purely without making the slightest change in color on the release. "I", as in "sky", is similarly a combination of "Ah" and "Ee" and cannot be pronounced any other way. "A" and "I" are rightly called diphthongs. They need attention in singing. The word "mine" is often sung "mah-een" with an equal lingering on both its parts, whereas the first part should have the lingering and the last part the slightest release effort when the word is completely finished. U is likewise a combination of "Ee" and "Oo" and should be sung with the tone on the *last* half of the combination.

Consonants, particularly those followed by "L" and "R", offer good opportunity for attack. The word "Glory" is a splendid word to begin a phrase because of the explosive character of the "Gl." Where "R" occurs in the first consonant combination, it should have the slightest of trill of the tongue. "Praise" will fairly spring forth from the mouths of a chorus if the "P" is struck, followed quickly by a slightly trilled "r."

Of recent years lingering on final consonants has become a serious factor in charlatan singing. Originally, vocal teachers spent much time teaching their pupils to sing the vowels. In fact the whole vocal technique demands this, because consonants cannot be sung with any tonal quality, being merely attack and release points of words. But someone, probably a radio stunt man, made great use of the humming of final consonants, particularly those ending in "n" and "ng". The effect of this humming the ending of every possible word, where it can be done, was indeed a rather striking and beautiful effect, particularly over the loud-speaker. But vocally this is of course only a stunt and does not represent good singing. Nevertheless many teachers of choral music promptly seized on this as an added "technic" for their choruses and we are still amazed to hear, even on Sundays, the village choir singing "Amen-n-n-n-n". Others have studied their song texts for every possible place where they may stop and put in a hum or two.

This practice is as perverse as it is ridiculous and should be done away with in all matters of good vocal technique and tonal production. The good old rule still stands: *Sing the vowels!* Any departure from this is usually for sensational and "show" purposes.

The general rule for good diction is to search carefully for the proper vowels and consonants to bring forth clearly, and then to inflect the proper word or syllable of a word.

Eloquence is delivery in proper style and mood.
Diction is delivery in proper clarity.
Inflection is delivery of words in proper accent.
Pronunciation is delivery of vowels and consonants in proper focus.

The pronunciation of Latin texts

There seems to be general confusion as to the proper method of pronouncing Latin texts, which are encountered, especially in the works of the older masters. Not even the books on this subject are all in agreement, one writer saying that there is no such pronunciation as the long E (pronounced AY) and others ignoring the use of the short O (as in money). The general usage in practice today is as follows:

A is almost always pronounced. AH
E is long and is pronounced AY unless it is followed by double consonants, when it is pronounced as the English short E (eh).
I is pronounced as EE except before double consonants when it is pronounced as English short I (in).

O is long and pronounced OH except before double consonants when it has the sound of O (as in money).

U is long and is pronounced OO (as in moon) except before double consonants when it is pronounced as the sound heard in the word "put". "Mundum" is thus "mu (as in 'put') -nn-doom".

GN (as in "magnam") is pronounced as NY ("mahnyam").

C and T before I and E are usually softened so as to sound almost like CH and TS respectively. Thus "cruce" is "croo (as in moon) -cheh" and "gratia" is "graht—siah" (with short I). Before A, O and U the C and T are hard. "Circa", for example is "syr-kah". "Cervus" is "chair-vu (as in 'put')s".

AE is not as long I in English but as long A (AY).

OE is the same, or approximately so, having the characteristic of the E. Thus "coelum" is "chayloom".

V is pronounced as English V, not as W.

Examples: Latin—Innocentes pro Christo infantes occisi sunt ab iniquo rege, lactentes interfecti sunt, ipsum sequuntur Agnum sine macula, et dicunt semper: Gloria tibi Domine.

English—in(as in "in")-noh-chen-tace proh Chri(short "i")s-toh in(short)-fahn-tace okcheesi su(as in "put")-nt ahb eeneequoh rayg(hard)eh, lahkte(short)ntayce in (short)tair-fek-tee sunt(as above), i(short)p-soom say-quu(as in put)ntur Ahn-yum see-neh mah-ku-la, eht deekoont sehm-pair Gloh-riah ti-bi (both short) Doh-mi-(short) neh.

It will be observed that I before B, N, P and T is often short. Final E is also sometimes long and sometimes short and no general rule can be given except that an unaccented syllable of such a nature, or one finishing a clause or sentence is usually short.

The general pronunciation used is thus not like the classroom Latin in general use. This classic language pro-

nunciation is too hard and not beautiful enough for singing, so the Italian pronunciation is more closely used.

The singing of Plain Song

When music is used which embodies the chant, it is
well to know the chant and how it is to be sung. Often
the publisher of the American edition has caused it to
be printed as a straight line of whole notes. Of course to
sing a chant in such a fashion is as incorrect as it is to
sing any melody in all whole notes, especially when the
melody is only a vehicle for a line of declamatory material which must be broken up into long and short
syllables of inflection possibilities. The line of whole
notes may give some idea of the *trend* of the melodic
chant but it will certainly not give the time values.
These are actually indeterminable and depend on the
text which is to be sung. In fact Plain Song or Plain
Chant is dependent on the text and exists as a vehicle
for it.

The versions in the Graduale Romanum (the official
Vatican text) as well as the versions used by the Bene-
dictines of Solesmes and the equally intelligent treatment by the Grenoble scholars all boil down to one
point, namely, that to sing the plain chant correctly one
must attend a school where the "traditional" way to
sing these chants is taught. It is as one who tried to sing
the actual notes of the recitatives in the "Messiah" being at the same time ignorant of the manner in which
these notes have been altered in the actual singing, often
being completely reversed or approached from above.

However, to one who has not the time to study in the
schools of the church and who must perforce at the same
time "carry on" in his work with choruses, singing as
many of the great masters as is possible, he will not
commit many mistakes if he considers the line of melody
given as a guide to the inflection of the sentence as
though he were *speaking* it. As the voice speaks a line
there are places of stress and rise of voice or lack of
stress and fall of voice. There are places where the subject passes hurriedly to the verb and the verb hurriedly
to the object. The intervening prepositions, adjectives,
and the like, are often passed over without stress. At or
near the end of a clause or sentence usually comes a
rising point and perhaps a place of deliberate hold
before falling to the ending point. Use the text then
first as spoken and then use the melodic line given as a
track on which this spoken text may run. Usually the
plain chant thus interpreted will prove to be quite ac-
ceptable and not too incorrect. Certain license is
afforded the speaker in chant. He may not sing it as he
has learned it even in his chanting school, for he feels
a certain inspiration often at the words he is singing
and may dwell longer or shorter on the various points
of turn. Therefore keep in mind the general *principle* of
the interpretation and the detail will often adjust itself.
To give examples in text would be folly for it is a matter
which does not adjust itself from printed texts but
from hearing and studying. However, the principle of
it can be understood and even the singing of it can be

done without great erring. Better this than not to sing it at all.

The singing of polyphonic music

Music of the old masters from Palestrina, Di Lasso, Byrd, Gabrieli, and the others down the centuries must be considered in the spirit of one who contemplates Gothic art rather than that of the canvas with color. Here is *design* rather than mass. Here is structural skill rather than colors and lightings. The singer who looks for "sugary" chords of a melodramatic nature in the music of these great men will be disappointed. Chorus directors should study this factor in the interpretation of such music. How often does one hear the most atrocious introduction of all sorts of dynamic gymnastics, a la modern idiomatic "expression"! This is sacrilege. The purity of style in the polyphonic masterworks is that obtained by considering the text first and all its import, the singing of phrase by phrase in horizontal line with rises and falls to fit the voice, the imitations of the same in the other voices rather than the attempt to build up points of chordal interest and the general subservience of body to spirit which is a component part of the mood.

Choruses which essay to do this type of music should have these important facts pointed out to them at the outset. Otherwise they will quickly make the remark that the music doesn't have any "punch", or no "good old barber shop chords" and other similar and perfectly natural expressions coming from the modern school of materialistic ballyhoo in music. One of the worst things that ever happened to sacred music and to all attempts to convey sacred messages by music was the advent of the so-called "gospel" song with all of its bar-room harmonies and jack-a-napes organ grinder rhythms. The chorus, however, as it grows in appreciation and understanding of the purity, depth and beauty of the great music of the polyphonic era, will eventually discover that no other type of music will prove quite as satisfying.

Musicianship of the conductor

It follows that choral conductors have much to do with their music besides handing the singers a copy and then standing up in front of them to "go through" it. Because choral conductors do not have to do instrumental music, they often by the nature of their training feel that even if they cannot read a score or direct a symphony they are at least capable of "teaching songs". The good choral conductor must be as good a musician, yes perhaps even better, than a professional symphonic conductor. He must have studied music both instrumentally and vocally, having put in long hours of hard practice and reading, attempting composition in various forms, and becoming as proficient as possible on some instrument. He must, after leaving his studies keep up with his work every day by playing, singing or studying scores; in short, living in the atmosphere of music. One swims by being in the water. Command of the musical range, understanding of how to do music, traditions and techniques, how to take beginners and inept people and make them better, proper interpretation of music whether marked by an editor or unmarked with even *tempi,* the "feel" of the music—these and many other things which are often thought to be "born in" musicians can also be considerably acquired. But it does require thought, study and experience. Choral directors must be good musicians!

CHAPTER XIII

THE PROGRAM AND THE CONCERT

Before a number is rehearsed it is assumed that the conductor has spent hours in search of proper music and that when the singers are ready he knows what the entire program is going to be. This is one of the precepts set forth in the section entitled "Preparation of the Chorus," page 68.

Planning the program

There are three types of programs. They are:

1. The chronological type
2. The mood or spirit of text and music
3. The contrast

Chronological type

Programs chosen because of their chronological significance, often begin with compositions of some of the old masters, coming down into modern schools of composition. This is the old-fashioned way and is still largely used. There is no more reason for beginning a program with Palestrina or Bach than there is to begin a dinner with a certain course, except that custom or desire to show evolutionary progress may dictate such

123

action. Therefore, a program planned on this basis must have definitely in mind a procedure from the old to the new without regard primarily to the text or the mood. At any rate these two things will be given second consideration as reasons for choice.

Mood type

The mood program would begin with some number that establishes a definite mood, at least for a certain part of the program, changing later to some other mood. For example, the first half of a program might be sacred, while the second half would be secular. To be more specific one might start with a number depicting the prophecy concerning the coming of Christ. This would be followed by a number about the birth and adoration. This in turn would be followed by a lullaby such as the one by Howells or perhaps a hymn to the Virgin. Now a chorus of heavenly hosts containing words of praise for the advent of the new Saviour can be introduced. Then such a number as Healy Willan's "Three Kings" would fit in nicely. This cycle would continue, depicting the words or teachings of Christ or it might digress into one of the episodes of his life. Candlyn's "Fierce Raged the Tempest", Noble's "Fierce Was the Wild Billow", or Hugh McKinnon's "Lord Christ Came Walking" would now fit into the program. This could be followed on and on to Christ's death and ascension. Such a program would be very interesting and contain all schools of composition from the old Italian to the modern English and American.

A conductor might use a small portion of such a cycle and thereafter switch to a secular group of numbers dealing with romantic subjects more or less related to each other.

Contrast type

The most successful type of program for present day use is that in which the various styles of musical works are set off in sharp relief against each other. A modern work of secular nature could be followed by a number like Morley's "Fire, Fire My Heart". They are so distinctly different even in style of articulation and tone quality that immediately the listener is pleasantly shocked. The modern urge is to get much variety and this kind of a program certainly offers the conductor the opportunity. It is not best to mix sacred with secular but to work gradually from one to the other.

The matter of contrasting keys must be considered as well as that of contrasting texts and moods. One number should not follow another in the same key. The key of C, for example, should be followed by some key which is situated farther from that key in the progression, such as the key of E, F, G, or A. This number should be then followed by one pitched in a correspondingly removed key. If it is apparent that two numbers simply must follow each other and that they are in the same key or very closely situated, the conductor must bend energy toward a distinct style for each of the numbers or he must have radically different means of interpretation of them. Otherwise the two numbers being close to each other in tonality will tend to wear the audience, all unconsciously to them.

Example of contrast program

The following is a program given recently by the Chicago A Cappella Choir:

Sing We Merrily Unto God .... Noss
The Three Kings .... Willan
Song of the Night .... Dunn
Fire, Fire My Heart .... Morley
Autumn .... Gretchaninoff
Sing Ye Unto the Lord (four movements).......... Bach
Intermission
Offering of the Soul .... Cain
Now is the Day of Resurrection .... Wood
Out of the Silence .... Jenkins
The Lonely Pine (arr. by Noble Cain)...... Rachmaninoff
The Gypsy Laddie (Kentucky Mountain Song)..... Malin
Let Thy Blessed Spirit .... Tschesnokoff
Wake, Awake .... Christiansen

Up to the Bach number each number was of definitely contrasting character. "Fire, Fire My Heart" coming after James P. Dunn's modern orchestra of the voices produced a startling change. Closing the group with the Bach number brought about an entirely different effect than it would have if it had been used to open the program. It requires about fifteen minutes to sing the four movements and it ends with a tremendous whirlwind finale. After the frivolities of the first group it was brought out that Bach was the greatest writer of them all. His great work brought forth prolonged applause, lasting continuously for about five minutes.

The last half of the program offered again contrast of both mood and key.

Length of the program

The choral program should not be too long. One hour is the limit. Let the singing begin at 8:30 and close about 9:40, allowing ten minutes for intermission. Let the audience leave the hall wishing that they might have heard more!

Critics

It is well to consider the probable visit of newspaper writers and to plan the program so that, regardless of their time of arrival or departure, they will hear one heavy number and one light number, or two styles of composition.

Soloists, assisting artists and guest conductors

It is felt quite often by many, in choosing program material, that the use of numbers requiring a solo voice is desirable. This may, in fact, be true and may add considerable interest to the program. Especially if the voices are pleasing and are drawn from the personnel of the chorus itself does this hold true for it causes more local interest. The introduction of soloists who are not members of the regular chorus is a matter which should be well thought over because the bringing in of such an "outsider" often causes an attitude of comparison both in the chorus and in the audience.

Perhaps the bringing in of an "outsider" as assisting

artist, guest conductor, etc., is done in order to give opportunity for publicity for the concert or to "fill the house" because of the acknowledged excellence or reputation of the performer. This point is certainly excusable, but it should be handled with care because the assumption is, although implied, that the chorus of itself cannot produce a program which is entertaining enough without the aid of these outside artists. On the other hand it may be a way to make the chorus better known to the community and result in vastly increased prestige for future concerts. In general it could be said that if assisting artists are to be used in any way the chorus should be drilled to a high state of perfection itself, so that if there is any comparison at all it will be in the interest of the choral work.

The mind of the audience

The program should be so arranged that it will appeal to any normal human being. It will not be so necessary then to consider the kind of audience which will be encountered. "Playing to an audience" may sometimes become necessary but as a rule the best performance, artistically and technically, will appeal to both the sophisticated and the uninitiated. The American public will applaud anything that is expert, whether it be in field of sports or of art.

Encores

It is a question as to the advisability of giving encores. Unless the demand become so insistent that the program cannot go on, no encores should be given until the end of the program. It is better to allow the most thrilling effect to remain in the mind of the audience, rather than attempt to produce it again. The second time it may not strike such fertile soil.

Stage effects

Concerts should be given in a well lighted hall. The house lights should not be turned off. They should be dimmed, if very bright, so that they will not glare into the eyes of the singers. No stage lights or effects should be attempted. Footlights are simply out of the question. The chorus must sing as if in normal surroundings. To attempt an approach to the operatic or dramatic in stage effect will detract from the message of the singers.

CHAPTER XIV

THE CONDUCTOR IN THE CONCERT

Use of the baton

A detailed account of the various positions and figures made by the baton in the conductor's hand will be omitted here since it has been adequately covered in good books.* A few words as to its general use are added.

The baton symbolizes mastery. Conductors should assume an air of complete assurance, confidence, mastery, domination of all that takes place. To project the person into such an attitude without the aid of some foil for his position is rather personal, both to singers and to audience. The baton, though only a small article, is large enough to hide this element of personal injection.

License of the baton

Beating of time with a baton is the least of its uses. The modern way to conduct a chorus is to use the baton primarily as a conveyor of ideas and, secondarily, as a time beater. Often the baton follows a phrase, placing the proper emphasis on the more important words or syllables of words, thus aiding eloquence, inflection and

---

* Notably in "The Eloquent Baton" by Will Earheart.

diction. Sometimes it disregards the conventional beating of time entirely and follows instead the rhythm or the accent. This is quite often apparent in recitative or chant.

1. The baton is used dynamically to draw the tone forth from the singers or to suppress the tone. See Dynamics, page 98. If not on a sustained chord the increased tone is indicated for the passage by the more vigorous beat. The opposite action is used for diminuendo in passage work; the beat becomes easier.

2. The baton can indicate blending or merging of tones by a slight horizontal waving while holding or during passage work. The movement should be as if the conductor were leveling off the top of a cup brimming over.

3. The baton indicates precision by the definiteness with which it may be moved. Staccato passages often are indicated by a bouncing quick movement up and down.

4. The baton can indicate a slur or a portamento. It often employs the same movement to indicate a smooth and high placement when approaching a high tone. This gesture is a graceful little loop over the top of the figure as if coming to rest on the spot from above.

5. The baton can indicate profundity by pointing down as if into an abyss, even while continuing its regular movement of beating time.

6. It can indicate sonority by being pushed at the singers as if there were resistance to it.

7. Attack and release should always be preceded by a preparatory movement of the baton slightly up and then the down or cross movement given. The attack movement is usually definitely downward, while the release movement is usually across the field.

8. One part can be pushed to the fore by a back-handed stroke although this is usually done with the left hand.

Use of the left hand

What the baton does in a broader way the left hand does in a particular or detailed way. The baton signifies action by the entire chorus with now and then perhaps one part to the fore. The left hand is used for individual parts and individual voices.

1. The left hand usually takes care of entrances of parts while other parts are singing.

2. The left hand signals for pitch ascendency or descendency.

3. It signals for roundness of tone or sharpness of tone.

4. For humming.

5. For closing the mouth or opening it and other smaller details of the interpretation.

A vernacular way of expressing the relationship of the left hand to the baton would be: The right hand plays the organ; the left hand manipulates the stops and combinations.

Personal carriage or behavior on stage

The conductor should walk to his place of conducting with a quick firm tread, without swing of the body or evidencing either fear or braggadocio. He must keep his personality buried in the baton and never "show off" in his body movements. Waving of both arms is seldom indulged in by an experienced conductor.

During conducting, the body should pivot and bend from the hips. The knees should not bend inward or backward. A few steps out of position toward the chorus or any section of the chorus may be permissible. These would occur as if the conductor were moving slightly nearer his singers in order to drive them unmercifully into the thick of the development of a complex section; or in receding from the chorus as if serene in the knowledge that the chorus is expertly rendering a passage with nonchalance. These movements must come naturally and as if inspired by the passage being given. Vigorous nodding of the head and displacement of hair which must needs be brushed back into place ever and anon by the frantic conductor is a thing amusing to behold and yet it is done by some of our best conductors in moments of forgetfulness.

Absolute control

Singers who are seated are in more perfect control than singers who are standing. Standing to sing a number is as much as stating to the audience "Now we are going to do something; watch us". The atmosphere of the perfectly balanced and well-planned program will be disturbed by the injection of the chorus-personality as much as by conductor-personality.

Second, the difference in height of individual singers is noticeable at once while standing, but not when seated, because the average person is the same height from the trunk up. Thus the appearance of the chorus is more uniform.

Third, the singers if leaning slightly forward and erect from waist up, can sing just as well as those standing. No muscles below the waist are used in singing. In fact choruses which stand are apt to use the muscles of the legs in shifting weight or position slightly, thus causing the picture on the stage to move in its individual parts.

Fourth, the chorus, while standing tends to pull away from the complete domination of the conductor. They feel, bodily, more free and by this fact often transfer the feeling into one of mental state. This gives the appearance of easier discipline. While seated the chorus cannot inject its personality with its physical freedom and discipline then appears to be strict. The consequent surety of attack and execution is materially strengthened.

Fifth, the blend of voices is better when sitting. In this position each row of heads is approximately on the same level. The sounds mix and proceed to the ears of the audience in a better focus.

Sixth, the standing of a chorus is physically wearing on the singers, especially the women who have foot wear in keeping with concert style. Choruses which have been on tour can recount their experiences with fatigue caused from the continued standing of the chorus for all numbers. Some numbers which are very long actually wear the singers to such a point that there may be extensive flatting. There is every reason to conserve the energy of the singers. Seating them is the best way to do it.

Lastly, the picture on the stage is not disturbed as it is when singers stand and seat themselves several times.

It is far better to train the chorus to sing properly when seated. This style is truly a cappella, non-personal, and produces the better musical performance.

CHAPTER XV

THE CHORUS IN RADIO BROADCASTING

Many things are to be considered when thinking of broadcasting a choir concert or a group of numbers by a choral organization. When radio was in its infancy, it was considered something of an honor to be asked to broadcast. There was also the fascination of being able to sing before a "mike" and to know that all the friends and admirers of the group were "tuned in". There was also the ever-present thought that in such a way the largest possible audience was available and this thought inspired many with its possibilities. Since the newness and novelty of radio broadcasting have worn off a bit, and the industry of radio has mushroomed into a mammoth commercial project organized for the purpose of making money from advertising on the air, it follows without any great amount of speculation that the purpose of a choir on the radio is subject to considerable doubt when it comes to either its necessity or practicability.

First of all, it is a common practice in radio to pay choirs nothing at all on programs which are called "sustaining" or "educational", the reasoning of the radio companies being that such choirs should be glad of the opportunity to appear. Just why they should be glad to work up program material into concert shape, as well as take the time and trouble to travel to radio stations, involving transportation expenses, the disruption of school or personal routine of several people, the acquirement of a studio often unfit for choir singing, being moved about here and there by a radio production man under the necessity of trying to get a good "balance" on the "mike", being denied the use of the regular choir accompanist because of some inexorable union rules that a strange pianist must either play or "stand by" (incidentally for *pay*), be given a time of appearance which is not good or which cannot be sold to someone else for advertising, furnishing thus free of charge for the radio station, a program which is to its own interest to have on the air, just why this should appeal to choral directors is not clear. While the schools are not organized for making money, it still would not be ungracious to give a school choir an honorarium of $50.00 to $100.00 for its school music budget or for its own purchase of choral music.

Is there anything wrong in this? Certainly not, especially when everybody in the broadcasting station from the janitor to the man in the front office is *paid*. It is a shameful lack of ordinary good taste to ask the schools, or anyone else for that matter, to broadcast without pay! Teachers with school organizations learning programs for school and concert purposes would do well to give this matter serious thought before they accept any invitations to broadcast. They certainly would not be "prostituting" their art in any sense by informing the radio stations and other agencies that the school would be glad to perform as a special feature for which it would expect to be paid, the money to go to its own music fund.

There is another reason why choral societies should not broadcast, even when paid for it. Due to the fact that the choir must be "picked up" and transmitted by a mechanical medium, it will never sound like itself when heard by the ordinary human ear. The best choirs in the world often sound disappointingly inadequate when put into a microphone, either for broadcast or for recording. The perfection of the transmitting mechanism is being constantly improved; the amount and qualities of overtones are being incorporated more and more into more "natural" sound, but the actual sound of the chorus will never be broadcast or recorded as it is, because it MUST go through a medium before it reaches the human ear. One very famous choir (and it is not my own) has already refused to make records or to broadcast because its director who happens to be honest, logical and consistent, and who cares nothing for commercialism or money in his hands, has said that his own reputation as well as his choir's suffers from records and broadcasts. And he is right! The Chicago A Cappella Choir, in my seven years of broadcasting with them, did hundreds of net-work broadcasts using from sixty singers to small groups of eight or ten singers, the majority of instances being with twenty-four voices, and it is a fact that this choir never did sound like itself! It often achieved beautiful results but it never sounded like it could or should have sounded. And this was at a time when I was personally interested in perfection of transmitting, microphone adjustment, and all the things that go to make up as good a broadcast as was possible.

Another very important reason for not waxing enthusiastic about broadcasts of choruses is that the radio companies reserve the right to determine what numbers can be performed! If these choirs are good enough to broadcast, it is not being unreasonable to assume that the material they provide and which they have often spent their own money to procure, should also be free from any such restriction on its educational or musical value!

But now, assuming that objectionable features have been eliminated and that the choral group is going to broadcast, certain methods of procedure are advisable. Let us discuss these:

First of all, the unaccompanied group: A general rule can be established that *in proportion to the size of the group the distance from the microphone increases,* up to the point of "room noise" or local sound leakage. This is true with all types of microphones!

The reason for this is, that starting with one voice and adding one at a time, as each voice is added another set of factors enters the picture aurally. Each individual voice has its characteristics of timbre and volume at any given placement of vocal production. Hence, the more close to the microphone, the more acutely these individual differences will be amplified. It is as if the conductor himself were standing right in the midst of his singers. He would hear individuals. If he should get some distance away he would begin to hear a blend of the ensemble. The problem then first is to secure a *blend*. This will be done by developing the *tone quality* of the choral ensemble, regardless of size, a quality distinct from the quality of the individual.

The choral blend is much easier to develop with groups of from three to eight singers when those singers sing softly enough to hear each other and to imitate each other. This type of soft blended tone is what is employed by the majority of radio vocal trios and other combinations. It usually does not come out of the loud speaker the way it is sung into it at all. It very often comes out quite loud and full, whereas the voices may be exerting the lightest possible tone energy.

When the number of voices begins to reach the proportions of a choir of from sixteen to sixty or more voices, this soft and crooning type must be abandoned for straight choral singing, with the ensemble blend dependent on the choral tone which the conductor develops as he tones down this voice and points up that voice, and so on, much the same as he would smooth out a choir of wood-winds or brasses.

As the size of the chorus increases and the microphone is moved away from them, there naturally arises a condition where it does no good to move the microphone any farther away. This point will be ascertained when the hollow echo of the room is heard, or other local noises leak into the microphone more strongly than the chorus tones. This is commonly called "room noise". It can also be heard when more than one microphone is being used and, for that reason, one microphone is productive of the best pick-up. When such noise is heard it is best to move the microphone toward the chorus again until it disappears. If, on doing this, the blend is not good, the microphone should be then moved up or down or sideways in an effort to pick up more of the part needed and to eliminate the part or voice not needed. It is not necessary to move the voices about! Moving the individual voices about destroys the regular concert position of the singers. It takes them away from the person by whom they are accustomed to sing and often produces disorganization and actual panic in performance. Neither will they be able to secure the same blend with the new alignment of voices. The conductor should insist that his choir stand or sit in its regular concert formation, familiar to him, to the individual singers and productive of the best results. Then treat the microphone as a mechanical ear (which in effect it is) and move this mechanical ear until it picks up the group at about its normal sound. The men may stand behind the women if they are accustomed to do this in concert. Moving the microphone up higher and pointing down is the same as raising the back rows of men up with risers, so the result should be the same. In no case should the choir's *regular* stance be disturbed. Many radio production men, particularly the more inexperienced ones, think that they must begin to move voices around here and there, placing and re-placing them in order to, as they say, "get a balance". Good radio production men never do this. They ask the choir to assume its normal concert position and then devote their attention and that of their accompanying engineer to picking up the chorus in the best possible way.

The discussion thus far has been relative to the unaccompanied chorus. When there is accompaniment to be considered there are of course some additional things to think about. First there is the matter of where the accompanying agent is placed and how much volume it entails. The general rule here given is that *in proportion to the mass of the accompaniment the chorus must be nearer the microphone.* This, of course tends to destroy blend. Most successful accompanying agents are those which are reduced to a minimum or consist mostly of high frequencies of vibration, such as violins. The lower and more "meaty" instruments will interfere with a good pick-up of the chorus. The answer to this is that where a full accompaniment, such as a full orchestra, is necessary, the singers must be placed near the microphone and be perhaps reduced in number, especially if there is not space to get the whole chorus near the microphone.

Where a piano alone is used to accompany the chorus, it must be placed somewhere in the studio where it will not be picked up louder than the chorus. This may be in the line at right angles to the chorus, or off to one side. But if it is right in front of a chorus the piano is very likely to be picked up first.

Returning to the question of more than one microphone: More than one can be used, of course, but they should be used to pick up spots or details which are to be added to the ensemble. For example, one microphone might be on the piano, especially if it has any sort of solo part to play, and another microphone might at the same time be on the chorus. But it would not improve anything to put one microphone on the sopranos, another on the altos, another on the tenors, and another on the basses, unless the chorus was of mammoth proportions, say a thousand or more voices. Even then, one microphone will give the clearest and best performance if the proper balance can be found with it. It must be remembered that the *volume* does not increase with more than one microphone. The level of the sound going out is the same, whether there be one or a dozen microphones open!

More than one microphone is often seen in radio studios during broadcasts and the general supposition is that they are all in use, whereas they are closed off by the engineer in his booth until they are needed for a particular "spot".

More than one microphone will also produce a condition called "out of phase". This is due to the fact that the sound travels to the microphone at a certain rate per second. It reaches one microphone at a different instant than it reaches another two or three microphones, all of them receiving the sound at slightly different instants. While this might not be detectible at first hearing, yet, amplified as the sound is on the microphones, it produces an effect in sound as of a picture out of focus. It is not as clear as it should be.

Perhaps the greatest complaint of musicians is that the radio makes the pianissimos loud and pulls the fortissimos down to a medium. This is quite true, as a general rule, and it will continue to be so until equipment is improved. The engineer in a radio booth, monitoring a program, gets much verbal abuse because he "does things" to the dynamics of music, yet he is only doing what is required because of the limits of the transmitter and of the lines carrying the program. Too great volume must be pulled down and music too softly done must be pushed up a bit or there will not be enough energy of the magnetic type to even get "out on the air". Conductors of radio groups, particularly loud ones, soon learn to modulate the tone of the group so that no great and ear splitting crescendos take place. The conductor might be helped in judging this by remembering that the microphone is an ear. A loud chord would not be shouted into an ear close up. The farther away the loud chord is from the ear the more possible is the reception. But when this is done, the soft chords must be correspondingly louder.

Summarizing: (1) Unaccompanied choruses broadcast best. (2) Distance from microphone increases with the number of singers, up to a certain point. (3) Accompaniment, if any, must be subservient to singers. Keep it soft or out of line with singers. (4) Singers should not be moved about from spot to spot in order to secure balance. (5) It is not good to broadcast at all under certain circumstances. (6) More than one microphone on any unit is detrimental. (7) Treat the microphone as an ear and modulate accordingly.

CHAPTER XVI

COMMUNITY VOLUNTEER CHOIRS

The Community chorus, or the chorus which is made up of members not particularly identified with any one type of educational institution; choruses such as the many and varied women's organizations in rural districts, the mother-singers, the father-singers, the associated glee clubs, and any and all such manifestations of the love of choral music in America are decidedly worth while. The teacher who finds himself elected to a position of responsibility in the school system or some other phase of city musical life should not ignore the possibilities which these organizations offer. They should be investigated, to say the least, if only from a purely selfish basis, not so much for any financial betterment which might accrue as for the influence in the community, so important to the teacher. Many choral directors, acting more or less on a social impulse and with a desire to become more fully established in their communities, have found that the acceptance of directorship in such musical organizations, even though amateur in the extreme, has, in some cases eventually developed into something very satisfying both musically and financially.

School choruses, in many instances, need some sort of outlet for graduates, where they may continue the work started in the regular school musical organizations. A good community choir or chorus offers an excellent opportunity for such "alumni" singers and once having been trained by the same director, it becomes a natural and logical procedure for the director to use many former graduates in such a chorus to very decided advantage. Again, such choruses generally predispose a community more or less favorably toward choral music in the community itself and thus attract good will toward the school activities.

As a general rule, the procedure with the actual learning and rehearsing process is about the same as already formulated elsewhere in this writing, with but few exceptions. (1) Such choruses are "volunteer"— that is, they are not under any compulsion as to being present or of even enrolling under the restrictional confines of any established institution. The members of such a chorus are not bound, except socially perhaps, to accept any rules or laws laid down for them by the teacher or the school. They enter and attend such a chorus of their own free will. They remain in it as long as they feel that they are enjoying it. (2) As an assortment of ages will make up the personnel, more leadership of the type based on the handling of human beings by making them *want* to do what is set out for them will become necessary. (3) The finances governing the operation of such a chorus must be provided for in some manner, preferably by having "dues" or some other form of mutual support for the purchase of necessary music and for the defraying of expenses which are bound to be incurred as the organization progresses.

These three points of difference, and there may be others, depending on conditions, make it necessary for all problems of attendance, discipline and finance to be self-imposed and mutually enforced. The prospective conductor should not accept any such assignment or organize one for himself until these three matters are thoroughly foreseen and considered, if possible to a point where the conductor has nothing to do with them whatsoever except as he may make them feasible by his own success in making the chorus rehearsals enjoyable. He should not have to worry about attendance, discipline or finance. Assuming that the director is a good musician who still knows how to be practical in reaching the hearts of people in music and how to give them music which they will like without going to the extreme of singing nothing but "popular" music, these other matters should be undertaken by an *organized* and functioning group of participating people.

Regardless of how splendid a musician the director may be and how well his chorus is organized from a functional standpoint, the director must realize that, despite his fondness for certain compositions which he considers will be "good" for the chorus, he must proceed slowly. If erring is to be done, let it be on the side of giving his chorus a large *variety* of music to sing. Many of such numbers may seem to be beneath the dignity of the director; many, to be sure, the chorus itself will smile at eventually in toleration of their early attempts. But the music must be such that it will run the whole gamut from the classical to the frankly melodious and easier things.

There must be accompanied music, perhaps quite a liberal amount of strong unison tunes, as well as *a-cappella* music. There must be a good proportion between secular and sacred texts, for it must be remembered that such a chorus as we have been considering is not, of itself, a religious organization. Directors who do not keep this flexibility of repertoire in mind will tend to undo much that has been accomplished in organization and good will.

If a community chorus once functions well and is trained musically so that it sings with anything approaching inspired results, there will be many demands on its time for the purpose of singing "concerts". All such requests should be examined and considered carefully from all angles. If the sponsor of the chorus happens to have been a wealthy person whose further good will is necessary and who has made the request to sing, it would be folly to refuse, even though the chorus might lack adequate preparation. It would be better in such cases to sing long passages even in unison, eight bars for the women alternating with eight bars for the men and then both together, singing chords here and there where they may be sung well, or making any other sort of improvisations to give a good concert, rather than to hesitate or to argue that they are not "ready" or that musically they are not where the director wishes they were. If the sponsor of the chorus is the city council or a politician who used his good offices to get the chorus started, it would be a good idea to find out if any of the influential "backers" had daughters, sons or other relatives who could be given a small line of a solo part, or even featured in a group of solos. If the leading citizen wrote a song, even though an atrocious one, arrange it for the chorus to sing, and then sing it with all the finish that can be given it! If there is blame for the quality of the song no discredit will reflect to the chorus. Everyone who hears it will know who wrote it, and the composer may collect the blame while the chorus receives the praise.

Aside from these and certain other equally important requests, there will be many invitations to sing, in fact so many that some requests will have to be politely, but firmly turned down. In such cases let the proposal be gone over thoroughly by a committee of the members whose duty it is to handle such circumstances. Usually the unimportant "dates" will show themselves for what they are and no harm will be done. The director, however, should not exert any great degree of opposition to such "dates", even on the grounds of musical unpreparedness. He will perhaps realize that he is a social as well as a musical leader and make the most of it. There may be other ways of doing such things, but none of them will result in "selling" the chorus to the community which is, very probably, of prime importance.

If the chorus is not organized, except merely to "get together" and sing for the mutual admiration of the

members, these conflicting difficulties will not result and
the director, perhaps, would be more happy to have his
chorus thus independent of other considerations, merely
singing a concert when and if he thinks the chorus is
ready for it. It would appear, however, that if the conductor is to make headway in a city or community, he
must be fully aware of his social responsibilities and
then try to adjust the cultural values to that position. It
is even possible to start a city chorus with a minstrel
show and ten years later finish an excellent season with
an all *a-cappella* concert, or with the giving of the
"Messiah". People must be led from simple beginnings
to more complex forms of appreciation! This applies to
the singers as well as the listeners, particularly where
the project is more or less new.

Old and established choruses have a problem of what
to do with aged and unsatisfactory voices of loyal members. It is of course essential that young, fresh voices
be added constantly. The natural "turnover" of personnel will cause the dropping out of many members.
It is better, under ordinary circumstances, to let all old
voices strictly alone and endeavor to temper them with
good tone quality suggestions rather than to make any
gesture whatever in discharging them from the chorus.
The resulting improvement to the singing excellence of
a choir, caused by dropping out old and "cracked"
voices [good folks who usually feel they can sing as well
as anybody else] will not balance the harm done in hurt
feelings to say nothing of professional and community
prestige. It is well for the conductor to remember that

the singer was good enough once upon a time to sing in that chorus; therefore, he is still good enough and the slogan "once a member, always a member" is most satisfactory in the long run.

Naturally, membership in such a choir should be determined at the start. If it is announced that "try-outs" are to be held and voices listened to by a committee (never by the conductor alone) some of the difficulties may be smoothed out. But, once accepted, a singer should be left alone except for advice or guidance, and that, very tactfully, with the majority of remarks on the subject addressed to the whole chorus and not to the individual. Keep in mind constantly that these people "volunteered" for this work and that they are in a sense the guests of the organization!

The writer has had perhaps more varieties of singers under his baton in a quarter of a century of choral conducting than the average person. Estimating all choruses, including massed high school and college festivals, convention choruses, out-of-door choruses, and the like, choruses numbering from 200 to 5,000 voices at a time, it is not an exaggerated estimate to say that in twenty-five years, a half million singers have sung with him— perhaps more. The most difficult case at first sight usually becomes the most casual. Let the *personal* estimate of singers give way to an impersonal consideration of the aim of the endeavor as a whole and troubles about *who* shall sing and *what* shall be sung will be largely dissipated. One singer within memory was sent to me as a member of a certain community chorus, a member who was a mental case! She had been confined at certain times to institutions for the treatment of such pathetic and disordered conditions. To be frank about it, I was at first completely astounded that any sponsor or influential person back of the chorus would attempt to use the chorus as an aid to her. At first thought, it was beyond all good comprehension. Being assured that the person was quite harmless took one of the palpitations out of circulation immediately. More thought on the subject led me to say to myself "Why not? After all, this chorus is for the GOOD of the community and if we are not here for our avowed purpose, we are hypocrites. It is even possible that by choral music and normal association with others, the poor soul might be helped along her wretched way through life". Well, with much trepidation, it was agreed. As far as was determinable, no harm was done musically to the choral numbers sung. The quality of the voice was what is colloquially described as "gosh-awful" but I soon was able, by gentle means, to encourage this singer to "take it easy." Not once in a concert did I hear her voice, yet she was there and evidently enjoying it. Her appearance was actually more normal than that of many singers seen in action.

The up-shot of it was, that her friends, who had asked that she be placed there originally told me afterwards, that she had experienced great mental improvement during that year in the chorus. After all, it *was* a community chorus. Perhaps some of our highly specialized choirs would do better service to humanity if they were not so "selective." It's just a thought.

Other points on community chorus development will present themselves:

(1) Secure all the rehearsal time possible, and let the committee on attendance enforce attendance for the required number of rehearsals. Community choruses fall down more often because of lack of attendance than for any other reason. In the midst of a busy world there will *always* be reasons for not attending. However, the rehearsal period should be set aside devotedly by the loyal member as a time when no other attraction, engagement, or anything except illness will take him away.

(2) Do not move around from place to place for rehearsal. Acquire the best available location, preferably with plenty of room and a high ceiling—and stay there. Most church auditoriums are splendid places in which to sing. It is not necessary to have a platform or risers for rehearsals. Let the singers sit in the regular congregational seats. Avoid lodge halls and other places which may be heavily carpeted, or may have low ceilings and narrow dimensions, regardless of how long a space is available. Seek for roominess and reflection on all sides, and above as well.

(3) Do not limit the size of the chorus. Allow as many to sing as are willing to come and pass the voice tests. Make these tests easy, inspecting mainly for bad quality only. Don't worry the applicant about sight reading. No two persons read equally well anyway, and

in a chorus of this type sight-reading ability will soon
adjust itself.

(4) Have all accepted members sign an agreement
setting forth their own liability in case of any accident
while chorus is being rehearsed or transported from
place to place for concert or tour of any sort. This is
important! Add any other stipulation deemed advisable
and have such a statement read and understood before
signing and formal acceptance.

(5) Set up a regular business organization and let the
chorus determine all matters having to do with its
proper functioning, including the management of receipts and expenditures. Failure adequately to arrange
this has also caused the downfall of many otherwise well
functioning groups. Particularly with regard to the
receipt of moneys from any source whatsoever, eventually a few members might insist that they have certain
equities or "rights" and may even go so far as to demand payment for their "services". Let this be understood at the very outset, and quite clearly. It may even
be incorporated into the agreement which is to be signed
when the applicant becomes a member. Such matters
as these seem amusing at times, particularly when dealing with old friends or neighbors, but it is amazing how
time can sometimes change the complexion of a situation. It is just good business sense to have it agreed
upon even with the best friend in the world. What is
written and signed is settled.

(6) Do not place any restriction upon members singing in any other similar organization so long as they

attend your rehearsals and concerts. All the outside
singing they do will cause no harm. Such an attitude on
the conductor's part will also eliminate any jealousy
and rivalry between the chorus and other community or
private groups, and is essential to healthy progress as
well as good community spirit.

(7) Set up now and then a social event, such as a
party or picnic which might take place after the rehearsal for the evening is finished. The chorus needs this
relaxation from time to time and a good spirit will
surely ensue.

(8) Let the aim of the chorus be the singing of good
music, whether the aim be immediate or for some time
in the future. Use all other considerations as a means
to this end.

CHAPTER XVII

THE CHURCH CHOIR

Church choirs are either entirely "volunteer," partly "volunteer," partly paid, or entirely paid. Perhaps the large majority of church choirs today is volunteer, with here and there a paid soloist or a paid soloist on each of the four parts, soprano, alto, tenor and baritone. For general functioning, this arrangement is the most satisfactory. The director is thus assured of at least one good voice on each part. These, in addition to singing solos when necessary, can always bolster the respective parts and ordinarily bring about more feeling of confidence on the part of the remaining singers.

The entirely volunteer group finds itself floundering helplessly at times, singing solos in unison as a makeshift, doing anthems which are relatively too low in musical value, or limited in other ways. The paid choir usually presumes a certain air of professionalism, but does not often react to the message of the church, or its gospel in the same manner as it would were it donating its services. This is to be expected, for, when it comes right down to it, all paid employees of the church do not, by the very nature of the case, have the same attitude toward the service as if they were doing the work without remuneration. No reflection on ministers of the gospel or ministers of music is intended. It would be interesting at times, however, to observe the amount of zeal inherent in certain of this class were their salaries suddenly done away with. But, allowing for training, which is entitled to recompense, it still can be said that the germ of religious devotion lies in the amount of work that can be had as a gift. And thus we find in every church many individuals who are willing and eager to serve in the capacity of choir singers.

As the great choirs of the world were derived from the church and its functions in divine worship, so also is some of the great, if not the greatest music derived. And perhaps next to the exposition of the gospel in speech by the minister or priest, stands the ministrations of the divine messages with music as the vehicle. In some ways music is more powerful than the spoken word in that personality is, or should be, subordinated to the text; for surely matters of a controversial or dogmatic nature are not found in harmonic and contrapuntal designs. One can attend church almost anywhere where there is a good music, and come away feeling much more equipped to meet the problems of the everyday life, providing he has not been disturbed by something said! How subtle therefore is the influence of good music in the liturgy, and how far reaching its effect! For that very reason the church choir director should strive to keep "personality" from appearing in either the music, or the performances of the singers.

The ideal choir would be one that was not visible. No

soloist to stand aloft with great authority and "render" a more or less traditionally done solo; no choir to stand with great flourish and celebrate the occasion of the minister's moment of banishment from the spot-light by the singing of a blatant anthem; no director with waving arms and baton to take the eye and the mind from the true purpose of the meeting—these and other equally peaceful ministerings to the soul can be obtained only by the concealment of the choir or by the training of choir, soloists, yes, and the director and organist, in that sublime art of impersonalization.

The ideal director in church is one who does *not* use baton, hands or head any more than is absolutely necessary. If the director is also organist, the situation is more ideal than ever because he can thus lead and guide his singers from mood to mood, and sentence to sentence, playing cues and improvising the proper preambles and interludes, now and then nodding for entrances and releases and only exerting himself into active motion of arms or hands in moments of necessity. If he is hidden from the audience, so much the better. For here the technique, even of the baton, is diametrically opposed to that used in the concert hall. Here worship is the motivating purpose; the musical performance is secondary and subservient. Were the same well trained choir taken into the concert field, the technique of concertizing and showmanship should be taught them as another and different rôle. For once out of the church, the best trained church choir and its director must forego, for the time being, the idioms of the church and develop a concert style. It can readily be seen that a good church choir *can* be also a good concert choir, but that the viewpoints in either case are different. The church choir, then, is a unit in itself and has its own peculiar bit to add to the service of worship. In doing so, it needs careful training both in music and in spiritual values, keeping itself impersonal at all times.

Technical and physical aspects of choir training are the same as for any other type of chorus already discussed. Aside from the fact that the *mood* of singing may demand more attention in order to obtain that detachment from the worldly, and sought for in tone as well as demeanor; other things are gone about in rehearsal and training in much the same way that any rehearsal is conducted.

Certain other aspects may be studied for the moment. The church choir has a peculiar relationship between singer and institution. Although not a school having at least a nominal jurisdictional or disciplinary influence, the church does have a marked silent discipline over its members. A church choir director cannot order his singers here and there on a' time-schedule of rehearsals according to a program devised in school fashion, but he will find that he has a certain power over his singers that will cause them to follow him implicitly. This kind of allegiance is perhaps better than the mechanical kind which occurs in school procedure, using the word "mechanical" in the sense that it is set up by administrative heads. The feasance given by a church choir member, though voluntary, is none the less lax in constancy.

Perhaps it is because it is based on the inner conviction that here is a service to Almighty God and not to man.

Again, the church choir does not depend, as does the community chorus, for its success on the general popularity of the chorus in the community. There is a sort of quasi-authority and organization already in a church choir which gives the director great confidence if he will develop it. Sacred music should have its greatest expositions here, better than in the concert lime-light. Here is where the great sacred masterpieces belong.

With these facts in mind it follows that the church choir director should start his choir work with the children of the church, whether he does it himself or through the offices of an assistant. The number of choirs in a church are proportionate largely to its membership. Churches even in small towns usually have no difficulty in establishing three choirs, one called a junior choir, one a choir of young people of high school age, and one adult choir. There is ample music to be found for all classes, in all degrees of difficulty. There would seem to be no reason then why such development should not take place, except for a lack of volunteer singers. The usual complaint is that there are not enough high school age people for a young people's choir and that therefore they should be and are incorporated into the regular adult church choir. This is often a true complaint and due largely to the fact that young people of the age mentioned are not often amenable to parental suggestion that they go to church for a choir rehearsal. Often the parents don't care too much about it themselves.

Methods for combating this lack of enthusiasm, however, is something which goes farther than the confines of this book.

A good director who is enthusiastic and well liked will often have no trouble in getting all the young people he wants. The junior choirs offer little trouble because children at that age will do what they are told with better spirit; and once they become interested in singing their unison, two or three part numbers, or interpolations in regular services, they take great pride in their work. They probably will never grow away entirely from church choir participation. The high school and college age is today the most difficult to interest, and this statement is heard on all sides and from all churches regardless of how much disciplinary and jurisdictional control the church may have. All admit, however, that much of the success of the young people's choir depends on the person who is directing and training it. There is a great work to be done here by the right people.

The type of music used is a very serious consideration. Regardless of denomination, there is no need for the use of musically inferior numbers. Popular tunes, such as Liszt's "Liebestraum," have no place in *any* church even though used with sacred words. The "Sextet" from "Lucia" is another anathema usually perpetrated on thousands of church goers, just because someone has found some sacred words which may "go with" the music. It seems a matter of amazement that so many do not have any finer distinctive appreciations for what is sacred and what is secular than to thus bring about an almost illicit marriage of the most romantic tunes with the most holy words. A new hymnal presents a few examples in things like the "Londonderry Air" and Brahms "Lullaby"! Committees which make up such collections for their constituents to sing, are to be censured—and severely. The writer once almost lost his "job" because he refused to play "The Rosary" for a singer to sing with sacred words which the pastor of the church had written! What is it that compels one to turn thumbs down on such material? The answer may be "heredity", "environment", "association", "early training" or a number of other things, but there still remains that still small voice of instinct which tells the choir director that his music *must* be sacred in its original concept. A good rule to follow is: "When in doubt, don't do it." There is ample good music of church lineage from chorales and motets to modern anthems. There is no need to drag into the sacred confines of the church the secular melodies of the day. If all the good music written from the time of Palestrina to and including J. S. Bach (about 250 years) were done, doing a different number *every day,* it would require over four hundred years to get through it all! And this does not even take into account the works *since* Bach, which include some of the finest church anthems of all time. True, the director may have to do a little *looking* for music, but then that is what he is supposed to do. Is it not?

A few features of the church choir which might be mentioned as being of value are:

(1) If possible, some sort of rehearsal should be held Sunday morning before the choir sings the regular service. It matters not how devoutly the minister may pray with the choir just before they start their work (a fairly well established custom in some places) their singing will be just as bad as before, in all likelihood, unless they have had some kind of Sunday renewal of acquaintance with the notes, combined with a chance to warm up their voices. All too often, there is a choir rehearsal on Thursday or Friday night and then the choir is given an approval for Sunday. By the time Sunday comes, many have forgotten the things they did in rehearsal, not everything, of course, but enough to mean extension of effort in order to sing well. There are also likely to be some differences in personnel. Perhaps someone is ill on Sunday morning or some other singer fails to get the correct instructions. There may be a difference in line-up or in seating arrangement. It is far better to get the choir together as early as possible, even an *hour* before hand. It wakes them up and puts them into a better mood physically as well as spiritually. It also avoids those well known last minute arrivals, and those late risers who enter the vestment room rubbing their sleepy eyes and hoping for the best.

(2) Do not attempt a processional unless the physical aspects of the building lend themselves to such an activity. Just because someone likes a processional, or because a minister might wish to heighten the impres-

siveness of the occasion, is no reason to require people
to come pouring out of a hatchway in some badly located
corner leading up to a choir loft, fall into step with
others staggering under the blows of realism in architecture, hold hymnals in a cherubic pose and finally
navigate the passageway under the entry door with
triumphant sweeps like fishing vessels coming back from
a day on the banks, all the while taking twenty minutes
to a song that ordinarily requires four.

(3) Try to inject responses wherever possible in co-
operation with the minister. It is possible that he will
break his pastoral prayer in three or four places so that
a short "O Lord, have mercy" could be sung one time,
"Hearken unto our petitions" the second time, "Purify
our hearts to do Thy will" a third time, all in the same
key or being part of one longer response, finishing with
an Amen *without* humming the final "n" longer than
necessary to release the word. Of course, if the minister
does this he must give the director a typewritten copy
of what he is going to say, at least the sentences just
before the expected response. Do not attempt such responses without a cue in advance. Otherwise there will
be long waits to know whether or not the minister is
ready and sometimes there will be interruptions. Such
responding, however, will add much to the service if
injected quietly and unostentatiously. Most ministers
will welcome this if it is done well.

(4) Attempt from time to time some antiphonal
work. There is usually a place in every church, even
though small, to which a quartet of ordinary voices may

be sent to sing a few bars of an anthem. Should this group be out of sight, it is especially effective. Soloists are not needed; just plain, untutored voices will make a deep impression. Anthems abound affording places where this may be done. It makes little difference whether or not the composer indicated such a departure in the score. Locate a place which will be well adapted to such an interpolation and have a voice or any set of voices sing it.

(5) Avoid humming in church. This is a distinctly secular effect. None of the great masters of church music ever used humming. They used texts and sang long passages *on vowels alone.* Humming, in the last analysis, is used only as a substitute for instruments in the support of another voice or to produce an effect of instruments. This is not necessary in church. It may be beautiful at times, but it generates an air of artificial unguency and suppressed emotional fervor of the sickish-sweet type, and suggests a romance with a background of Hawaiian guitars, rather than the worship of the divine Creator.

(6) Organize the choirs with regular sets of officers and let them function so that they operate as much of the choir and its activities as is possible to turn over to them.

(7) From time to time have social meetings and keep the choir well acquainted and individually happy.

(8) Keep in mind that the church is, if anything, more important than the school or the home and that the

wise director of a school choir or of a community choir will also avail himself of the opportunity to serve in a church, no matter how small, if he is given the opportunity. If he is an organist or pianist, so much the better. He will then be able to have more mechanical equipment to work with and may spend hours playing the organ and generally improve his own musicianship.

APPENDIX I

SPECIAL SEATING PLANS

On occasion, special seating arrangement must be prepared. This happens when the choir sings a multiple chorus or a motet or madrigal for more than two choirs. The same principle of division holds here, namely, that of keeping the choir as a single unit in contact with the individual units into which it has been divided for the occasion.

The Tallis Motet

For the singing of the Tallis Motet for forty parts, eight choirs, which is the most elaborate choral work written, various arrangements have been used. Dr. Whittaker, in his performance of this work in 1929 with the Newcastle upon Tyne Bach Choir used the division on the following page (Chart No. 7).

This arrangement has a disadvantage in that Tallis wrote the motet for four *pairs* of choirs. The proper collaboration of these pairs is not possible in Dr. Whittaker's arrangement, good as it may be from other viewpoints. A thorough study of the plan of the Motet has led to the conviction that choirs 1, 2, 7, and 8, work more or less together and are *opposed* to choirs 3, 4, 5, and 6.

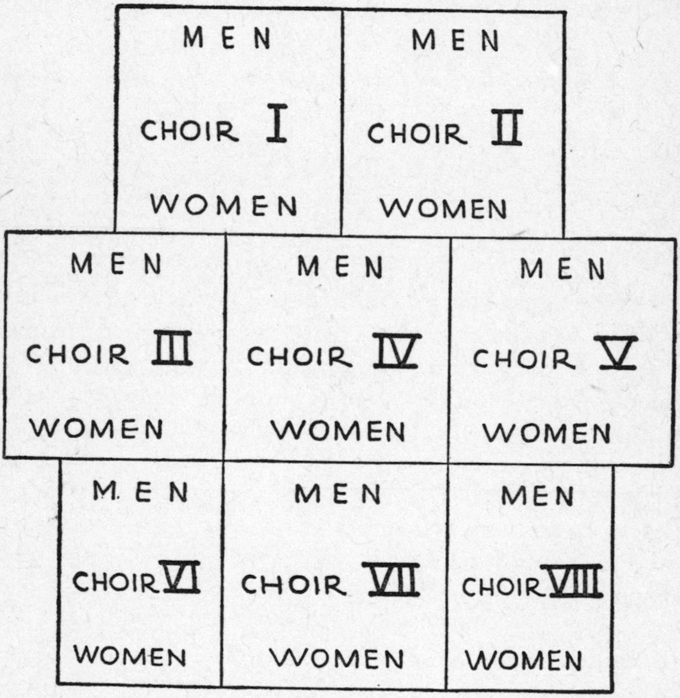

MEN	MEN
CHOIR I	CHOIR II
WOMEN	WOMEN

MEN	MEN	MEN
CHOIR III	CHOIR IV	CHOIR V
WOMEN	WOMEN	WOMEN

MEN	MEN	MEN
CHOIR VI	CHOIR VII	CHOIR VIII
WOMEN	WOMEN	WOMEN

CHART No. 7

The seating arrangement of the Chicago A Cappella Choir in its performance of this work for the first time in America in 1932, was as follows:

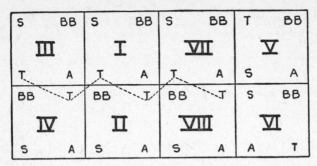

CHART No. 8

Analysis

My first reason for placing the singers in this fashion was that Tallis has the choirs enter one after the other, beginning with choir 1. Glancing at the diagram, it will be seen that the entrances of the choirs will appear (to the audience) to move from the center-top to the center-bottom on the left of the middle, then to the left-top and down to the left-bottom. It then abruptly switches to the other wing of the choir at the right-top, down to right-bottom and finally, back to the center-top and center-bottom on the right of the middle. This gives a maximum of antiphonal effect.

Secondly, at the 36th measure, while choirs 7 and 8 in the right-center are finishing a contrapuntal figure and while the other choirs are silent, choirs 3 and 4 are introduced for a few measures of solid block-harmony, in opposition to the counterpoint of the 7th and 8th choirs. Choirs 3 and 4, being separated from 7 and 8 and on the extreme left side, can bring this in as a totally different and separated unit.

When 3 and 4 are finished, 7 and 8 are still to be heard finishing their contrapuntal figure, which, in turn, ushers in a solid section of all eight choirs in semi-counterpoint and semi-harmony. This lasts for a few measures only, when once more out of this block is heard the 7th and 8th choirs beginning a re-trace of the process used at the beginning. The choirs now follow each other in reverse order back to the first choir.

At the 69th measure all choirs again sing, this time in contrapuntal style, but on ceasing the solid block, choirs 5 and 6 are heard continuing, paired, and stopping at precisely the same measure. This ushers in 1 and 2, paired, followed by 3 and 4, paired, then 5 and 6, paired, and finally 7 and 8, paired.

At about the 90th measure several solid blocks of harmony without counterpoint appear! In this, choirs 1, 2, 7, and 8 work against and antiphonally to 3, 4, 5, and 6. There is finally a pairing of 1–2, 3–4, 5–6, in that order and working back in reverse order immediately to a complete and dramatic pause on the word "respice". After this all choirs join in a solid and simultaneous block of harmony for just a few measures. This leads without stop into a most intricate and astounding solid block of counterpoint with all choirs singing together to the end! It is truly a masterful piece of musical architecture and it demands especial arrangement for proper performance.

Now as to the arrangement of the singers within the choirs: After a careful study of the entrance of parts, as distinguished from entrance of choirs, I determined to throw the tenors of choirs 1, 2, 3, 4, 7, and 8 together as nearly as it could be done, while in choirs 5 and 6 it seemed best to throw the sopranos together. This brought about a powerful display of the tenors, since they were in a horizontal placement right through the center. Tallis made abundant use of the tenors and developed perhaps the most beautiful figures and dramatic sequences between the various tenor parts than between any other parts. In choirs 5 and 6, however, he threw boldly into view the two soprano voices. All the other parts are criss-crossed, as will be seen from the diagram. Although they are separated from each other they are brought into the picture, as Tallis no doubt intended they should, in antiphonal style.

This rather lengthly discussion is given so that the art of properly placing a choir may be brought to the fore. Such things are matters of opinion and practice on the part of different conductors. It is evident that the proper placing of any choir requires much thought. All is not "hit or miss" in true *a cappella* singing. A definite motive must be discovered, first in the composition and then in the placement of the parts to properly expound the composer's idea. It is much the same as the proper disposition of troops on a field to obtain a definite objective. As in chess there are so many different culminations of the first few moves, so in the outcome of many concerts will different effects be noticed. Just "singing" a number is very elemental. It must be interpreted, dramatically, and with intelligence.

CHORAL LITERATURE

The material included in this list has been carefully selected from several thousands of compositions and is recommended for guidance in study as well as for public performance. Since there is an increasing demand for choruses which will fill the needs for festival occasions, employing mixed choral groups as well as those of women and men separately, it has been deemed well to include examples of all classes.

This list includes both *a cappella* and *accompanied* types of choral works. All titles preceded with an asterisk (*) indicate that the number is a cappella.

Where there are several editions of the same number, the work which has the most singable text or, for various other reasons, seems best adapted to good choral practice, has been listed.

Key to publishers:

AMP   Associated Music Publishers, 25 West 45th St., New York City.

AUG   Augsburg Publishing Co., 425 So. Fourth St., Minneapolis, Minn.

B&H   Breitkopf and Härtel, (see Associated Mus. Pub. above).

BFW   B. F. Wood Music Co., 88 St. Stephen St., Boston, Mass.

BHB   Boosey, Hawkes, Belwin, 43 West 23rd St., New York City.

BM   Boston Music Co., 116 Boylston St., Boston, Mass.

CCB   C. C. Birchard & Co., 221 Columbus Ave., Boston, Mass.

CF   Carl Fischer Inc., Cooper Square, New York City.

CFS   Clayton F. Summy Co., 321 So. Wabash Ave., Chicago, Ill.

CUR   Curwen Co., c/o G. Schirmer Inc., 3 East 43rd St., New York City.

FS   H. T. FitzSimons Music Co., 23 E. Jackson Blvd., Chicago, Ill.

GHM   Gamble Hinged Music Co., 218 So. Wabash Ave., Chicago, Ill.

GS   G. Schirmer Inc., 3 East 43rd St., New York City.

H&M   Hall and McCreary Music Co., 434 So. Wabash Ave., Chicago, Ill.

HF   Harold Flammer Inc., 10 East 43rd St., New York City.

HWG   H. W. Gray & Co., 159 East 48th St., New York City.

JF   J. Fischer & Bro., 119 West 40th St., New York City.

NAK   Neil Kjos Music Co., 14 West Lake St., Chicago, Ill.

NOV   Novello & Co., H. W. Gray, (see above).

OD   Oliver Ditson Co., 1712 Chestnut St., Philadelphia, Pa.

Ox   Oxford Press, c/o Carl Fischer Inc. (see above).

RAH   Raymond A. Hoffman Co., 509 So. Wabash Ave., Chicago, Ill.

WIT   M. Witmark & Sons, R.C.A. Bldg., Rockefeller Center, New York City.

It will be understood that the following list is one of outstanding examples of music under the respective schools rather than any attempt to formulate a complete list.

For mixed chorus

Gregorian Plain Song

*O Sons and Daughters..............Traditional   WIT

Early Netherlands School

*Echo Song ....di Lasso   OD
*Echo Song (better text) ....di Lasso   NAK
*Timor et Tremor ....di Lasso   WIT
*Ave verum Corpus ....Des Près   NAK
*Hodie Christus natus est..............Sweelinck   NOV

Italian School

*Jubilate Deo ....Gabrieli   NAK
*Tenebrae factae sunt................Ingegneri   WIT
*Tenebrae factae sunt................Ingegneri   CFS
*Adoramus Te ....Palestrina   WIT
*Exultate Deo ....Palestrina   WIT
*O che Splendor ....Palestrina   BM
*Response No. 3 ....Palestrina   HF
*Madrigal ....Sarti   CCB

English—Sixteenth Century

*Ave verum Corpus ....Byrd   WIT
*Misereri mei ....Byrd   BHB
*Come again sweet Love ....Dowland   WIT
*Dainty Fine Bird ....Gibbons   CCB
*Hosanna to the Son of David ....Gibbons   WIT
*April is in my Mistress' Face ....Morley   HF
*Fire, Fire my Heart ....Morley   H&M
*Since first I saw your Face ....Morley   WIT
*Sing we and chant it ....Morley   WIT
*Ascendit Deus ....Phillips   NAK
*Messenger of the Delightful Spring ....Pilkington   Ox
*In these delightful pleasant Groves ....Purcell   WIT

*Thou knowest Lord ....Purcell   OD
*In the merry Spring ....Ravenscroft WIT
*Mother, I will have a Husband ....Vautor BHB
*Alleluia ....Weelkes   Ox
*Adieu, sweet Amaryllis ....Wilbye   H&M

Spanish—Sixteenth Century

*Ave Maria ....Vittoria   WIT

Early German and French

*Blessed Redeemer ....Bach   WIT
*Come O Lord with Gladness ....Bach   WIT
*Now let every Tongue adore ....Bach   NAK
*King of Heaven ....Bach   WIT
*Sleep of the Child Jesus ....Gevaert WIT
*Joyous Christmas Song ....Gevaert WIT
 Amen Chorus ....Handel   CFS
*Adoramus Te ....Mozart   NAK
*Lo, what a beauteous Rose ....Praetorius WIT

Later German and French

*IIow lovely is Thy dwelling Place ....Brahms BFW
*O Saviour burst the heavenly Bound ......Brahms GHM
*The King and the Star ....Cornelius   WIT
*O Death, thou art the cool Night ......Cornelius NOV
 O Lord most Holy ....Franck   BM
 O Lord most Holy (better text) ....Franck   NAK
*Ave Maria ....Liszt   RAH
*Benedictus ....Liszt   HF
*Christmas motet ....Arnold Mendelssohn   GHM
 All choral works ....Arnold Mendelssohn   B&H
 All choral works ....Felix Mendelssohn   any
*Ave verum Corpus ....Mozart   WIT
 Prelude to "The Deluge"...........Saint-Saëns   WIT
 The Swan ....?.Saint-Saëns   HF
*Emitte spiritum Tuum ....Schuetky   NAK

Nineteenth and Twentieth Century English

*In the Wilderness ....Bainton	Ox
*I sing of a Maiden ....Bax	Ox
All Creatures of our God and King ......Chapman	CCB
*The Splendor falls ....Delius	Ox
*As Torrents in Summer ....Elgar	any
*Lullaby of Life ....Leslie	HF
Hail gladdening Light ....Martin	NOV
*O Bethlehem ....Murray	Ox
*There is an old Belief ....Parry	CCB
*When Allan-a-dale went a-hunting ....de Pearsall	WIT
*In dulci Jubilo ....de Pearsall	WIT
*The Second Crucifixion ....Sargeant	Ox
The Long Day closes ....Sullivan	WIT
*Bethlehem Night ....Warrell	Ox
*How eloquent are Eyes ....West	NOV
*Hail gladdening Light ....Wood	CCB

Nineteenth and Twentieth Century Russian

*Blessings of Peace ....Arkhangelsky	WIT
*Cherubim Song ....Arkhangelsky	WIT
*Hear my Supplication ....Arkhangelsky	WIT
*Incline Thine Ear ....Arkhangelsky	WIT
*Out of the Depths ....Arkhangelsky	WIT
*We have no other Help ....Arkhangelsky	WIT
*Communion ....Balakireff	WIT
*Send forth Thy Light ....Balakireff	H&M
*Cherubim Song No. 7 ....Bortniansky	WIT
*Glory to God ....Bortniansky	WIT
*Cherubic Hymn ....Gretchaninoff	NAK
*Holy radiant Light ....Gretchaninoff	GS
*Nunc dimittis ....Gretchaninoff	WIT
*Autumn ....Gretchaninoff	HF
*Hymn to the Virgin ....Gretchaninoff	RAH

*Communion Service . . . . Gretchaninoff   RAH
*Praise the Lord with a Song . . . . Kalinnikoff   CCB
*Hospodi Pomilui . . . . Lvovsky   WIT
*Clear and calm was that holy Night . . . . . Nikolsky   WIT
*Come praise the Lord . . . . Nikolsky   WIT
*Cherubim Song . . . . Panchenko   WIT
*O Lord we praise Thee . . . . Rachmaninoff   BHB
*To Thee we sing . . . . Schvedoff   WIT
*Sunrise . . . . Tanieff   HF
*Father, may Thy Children . . . . Tschaikowsky   WIT
*Cherubim Song No. 6 . . . . Tschaikowsky   NAK
*O blest are They . . . . Tschaikowsky   GHM
*The Angels' Song . . . . Tschesnokoff   WIT
*Let Thy holy Presence . . . . Tschesnokoff   CCB
*Thou Life of Life . . . . Tschesnokoff   NAK
*Repentance . . . . Tschesnokoff   WIT
*Now we sing Thy Praise . . . . Tschesnokoff   BHB

American and Canadian Examples

In many cases, the composers mentioned have written literally dozens of original compositions and arrangements. The writer himself has at this time (1941) approximately five hundred published works. Healy Willan of Canada, and in the United States such leaders in the field as Eric Delamarter, Joseph Clokey, Philip James, Don Malin and F. Melius Christiansen have contributed excellent choral works too numerous to mention. A few outstanding examples of the more attractive or useful works are listed here:

*Hymn to Music . . . . Buck   HF
*Deep River . . . . Burleigh   GS
 Fierce raged the Tempest . . . . Candlyn   GS
*Lost in the Night . . . . Christiansen   AUG
 Hymn exultant . . . . Clokey   HWG
*Alleluia . . . . Collin   GS

*June Moonrise ....Delamarter   HWG
O Lord, Thou art our God ....Dickinson   HWG
*Song of the Night ....Dunn   JF
When the Heart is young ....Gaines   OD
*Ballad of the Trees and the Master ....James   OD
*Glory to God in the highest ....Jones   CF
*Prayer ....Kountz   HWG
*Reflections ....Lawrence   CF
Dirge for two Veterans ....Lockwood   WIT
Dancer of Dreams ....Loomis   WIT
*Open our Eyes ....MacFarlane   GS
Let all the World in every Corner ....Malin   CCB
*Take O take those Lips away ....Moore   GHM
*Sunset ....Mueller   GS
The risen Lord ....Sowerby   BM
*The three Kings ....Willan   HWG

Examples of Choral Material by Noble Cain
Concert (difficult to moderately difficult)

*Say thou lovest me   GS
*Ode to Solitude   CCB
*The Splendor falls   HF
*O Thou in whose Presence   GS
Christ in the World (oratorio)   CF
God of the open Air   BHB
*O Watchers of the Stars   H&M
*Rarely comest thou   RAH
*Wake up sweet Melody   GS

Moderately difficult to easy, including encores and generally
recreational material

Ode to America   HF
America my own   HF
*Hymn to the Night   RAH
*My Dream is of an Island Place   GHM

*Roll Chariot roll (arr.)   HF
*O Susannah (arr.) Foster   IIF
The Long Day closes (arr.) Sullivan   WIT
*Ezekiel saw de Wheel   BHB
*De new born Baby   CCB
*Swing low sweet Chariot   FS

Selected examples of arrangements other than mixed

Lullaby (SSA)   HF
The Siesta (SSA)   HF
The Year's at the Spring (SSA)   HF
Ah Love, but a Day (SSA)   HF
De Gospel Train (TB or TTBB) (arr.)   HF
*Indian Serenade (TTBB)   RAH
*Come to me in my Dreams   H&M

Examples of medium difficulty for festival, church, or community without classification as to school of composition

For Mixed Chorus

*Send forth thy Light ....Balakireff   H&M
*Phyllis ....Brahms   WIT
*Blow, blow thou winter Wind ....Cain   HF
*The Cloud ....Cain   BHB
Lead kindly Light ....Cain   HF
Music when soft Voices die ....Cain   HF
The Night has a thousand Eyes ....Cain   HF
As from the Sun a Ray ....Caldara   WIT
Jesus, Saviour pilot me ....Clement   HF
Just as I am ....Clement   HF
Rock of Ages ....Clement   HF
O Loving Saviour ....Clement   HF
Friend ....Davies   BHB
O Lord most Holy ....Franck   NAK
*Russian Dance Song ....Gnotov-Krone   WIT

*Fair Maidens come forth .... Gnotov-Krone   WIT
*The two Paths .... Gretchaninoff   WIT
 If my Songs had Wings .... Hahn   H&M
*O Come let us sing .... Jans   BFW
*The Cossacks' March .... Arr. Koshetz   WIT
*A Violin is singing in the Street ...... Arr. Koshetz   WIT
*White Birches in the Rain .... Loomis   NAK
 Let all together praise our God .... Malin   CCB
 Now thank we all our God .... Mueller   GS
*Come praise the Lord .... Nikolsky-Krone   WIT
*Northern Lights .... Palmgren   WIT
 In the Time of Roses .... Reichardt   CFS
*Song for Evening .... Schmutz   WIT
 O my Soul bless God the Father .... Arr. Simes   BFW
 Song of America .... Southey   CFS
 All hail the Power of Jesus' Name ... Arr. Williams   Ox

For Men's Chorus

 Break, break, break .... Andrews   WIT
 Feldeinsamkeit .... Brahms   WIT
 Serenade .... Brahms   WIT
 The Sailor so trusty .... Bononcini   WIT
*Media Vitae .... Bruch   GS
*On the Sea .... Buck   NAK
*Come to me in my Dreams .... Cain   H&M
 Ezekiel saw de Wheel .... Arr. Cain   BHB
 God of the open Air .... Cain   BHB
 Hoodah Day .... Arr. Cain   HF
*Indian Serenade .... Cain   RAH
 Rhyme of the Country Road .... Cain   GHM
*Shadow March .... Cain   H&M
 Song of the Jolly Roger .... Candish   GS
 My Heart is victorious .... Carissimi   WIT
 The Road is calling .... Clement   HF
 Friend .... Davies   BHB

White in the Moon the long Road lies ....Fox   CF
Home coming ....Grieg   WIT
Hallelujah Amen ....Handel   HF
Down the open Road ....Haney   BFW
When the Bugles call ....Haney   BFW
In my Dreams I sorrowed ....Huë   WIT
General William Booth enters into Heaven..James   WIT
*The Choomack ....Arr. Koshetz   WIT
*The Cossack ....Arr. Koshetz   WIT
A hunting we will go ....Kountz   WIT
Good night my Love to thee ....Kountz   WIT
*Softly at Nightfall ....Kountz   WIT
Song of Farewell ....Kountz   WIT
To the Sea ....Kramer   WIT
*The Blue Birds ....Leontovitch   WIT
*Hospodi pomilui ....Lvovsky   WIT
*Sour Wood Mountain ....Malin   GHM
*Where lies the Land ....Malin   CCB
My River Home ....Moulton   HF
*Song of Love ....Palmgren   WIT
Heart of mine (Minnelied) ....Reger   WIT
Sunrise on the Ganges ....Scarlatti   WIT
*All through the Night ....Arr. de Brant   WIT
The Vagabonds ....Thomas   CF
Noël, Noël ....Arr. Grayson   NAK

For Womens' Chorus

A Prayer of Thanksgiving ....Allitsen   BHB
Assumpta est Maria ....Aichinger   WIT
God my King ....Bach   WIT
Now praised be the Lord ....Bach   WIT
Beauty is born ....Blakeslee   WIT
Sing Songs of Joy ....Bohemian-Grayson   NAK
Far and Wide ....Brahms   WIT
Ah Love but a Day ....Cain   HF

April Morning .... Cain	BHB
Bed in Summer .... Cain	BHB
In the silent Night .... Arr. Cain	OD
Lullay my Jesu .... Cain	HF
The Robin in the Rain .... Cain	GHM
Just as I am .... Clement	HF
The Chime .... Debussy	WIT
The Valleys of Dreams .... Fletcher	NOV
Beautiful Dreamer .... Foster	NAK
Come with thy sweet Voice again .... Foster	WIT
Lullaby of the Infant Jesu .... Gevaert	CFS
O divine Redeemer .... Gounod	H&M
A Birthday .... Horton	WIT
Pirate Dreams .... Huerter	OD
Childrens' Prayer .... Humperdinck	WIT
O press thy Cheek .... Jensen	H&M
Singing to my Love .... Justis	BFW
*Lullaby .... Arr. Koshetz	WIT
I'm only Nineteen (Kentucky Mountains)	
Ky. Mountain-Winter	CFS
Plaint .... Arr. LaForge	WIT
Scotch Christmas Carol .... Lamont	NAK
Come little Maid .... Luvaas	NAK
The Hills of Dream .... Malin	CCB
I waited for the Lord .... Mendelssohn	BHB
*The Shepherdess .... Roberton	CUR
Ship of Dreams .... Rowley	CUR
I walked through the flowering Forest ..Schumann	WIT
O dearest One, thou hast my Heart.Schumann-Cain	HF
*A widow Bird sat brooding .... Sharman	Ox
My Lover is a Fisherman .... Strickland-Cain	OD
Lullaby .... Simes	BFW
I heard you go by .... Wood	BHB

APPENDIX III

BIBLIOGRAPHY

(One hundred selected books for the Choral Conductor.)

The appended list of books contains many which are valuable additions to the conductor's library. Many of these books contain ideas which are in opposition to each other. By a study of conflicting ideas is one able to acquire and adapt to himself a style which is distinctively his own. By all means, let no one base his thought on the writings of one man! By a general summation and juxtaposition of conflicting ideas will general culture be attained.

Those marked * are recommended as valuable for reference work. ** means especially recommended.

Aesthetics, Psychology, and Science

** *Adolescence*, by G. Stanley Hall; Appleton and Co., New York, 1904.

Beautiful in Music, The, by Hanslick; H. W. Gray & Co., New York, 1881.

Effects of Music, by Schoen; Harcourt, Brace & Co., London, 1927.

Fundamentals of Psychology, by Pillsbury; Macmillan, New York, 1920.

Harmonics of Aristoxenus, by Macran; Oxford Press, London, 1902.

Heritage of Music, The, by Foss; (essays by nine men) Oxford, 1926.

* *History of Aesthetics*, by Bosanquet; Macmillan, New York, 1917.

Language of Color, The, by Luckiesh; Dodd, Mead & Co., New York, 1918.

Mechanics of Singing, The, by Evetts and Worthington; Oxford, 1928.

Music, a Science and an Art, by Redfield; Oxford Press, 1930.

* *Outlines of Philosophy of Art*, by Collingwood; Oxford, 1925.

* *Psychology*, by James; Henry Holt & Co., New York, 1923.

Psychology of the Emotions, by Ribot; Scribner's, New York, 1911.

Psychology of Singing, by Taylor; Macmillan, New York, 1908.

** *Science of Musical Sounds, The*, by Miller; Macmillan, New York, 1922.

** *Science of the Voice*, by Stanley; Carl Fischer & Co., New York, 1929.

** *Sensations of Tone*, by Helmholtz; Longmans Green, London, 1912.

Textbook on Sound, by Barton; Macmillan, New York, 1922.

* *Theory of Beauty*, by Carritt; Macmillan, New York, 1914.

Theory of Educational Procedure

Behaviourism, by Watson; Henry Holt & Co., New York, 1925.

Boy Voice, The, by Curwen; L. Curwen, London, 1894-1898.

The Child Voice, by Behnke and Brown; Ditson & Co., Boston, 1885.

Child Voice in Singing, The, by Howard; The H. W. Gray Co., New York, 1895.

Class Singing, by Whittaker; Oxford Press, London, 1925.

** *Development of Intelligence*, by Binet; Williams & Wilkins, Baltimore, 1916.

** *Educational Psychology*, by Thorndike; Columbia U., New York, 1926.

* *The Junior High School*, by Koos; Ginn & Co., Boston, 1927.

The Junior High School, by Smith; Macmillan, New York, 1925.

Mental Development in Child and Race, by Baldwin; Macmillan, New York, 1895.

* *Mental Growth of the Pre-School Child*, by Gesell; Macmillan, New York, 1925.

Music and Boyhood, by Wood; Oxford Press, London, 1925.

* *Principles of Secondary Education*, by Monroe; Macmillan, New York, 1914.

Psychology of Early Childhood, by Stern; Warwick & York, Baltimore, 1914.

Psychology of Musical Talent, by Seashore; Silver Burdett, New York, 1919.

** *Psychology of the Pre-School Child*, by Baldwin; Appleton, New York, 1924.

Text-Book of Experimental Psychology, by Myers; Longmans Green, New York, 1927.

Voice of the Boy, by Dawson; Laidlaw & Co., Chicago, 1919.

Practical Choral Work

* *Art of the Singer*, by Henderson; Scribner's, New York, 1906.

* *Art of Singing*, by Shakespeare; Ditson, Boston, 1910.

** *Bach's Cantatas*, by Whittaker; Oxford Press, London, 1924.

Choral Music, by Meese; Chas. Scribner's Sons, New York, 1901.

Choral Technique and Interpretation, by Coward; Novello, London, 1914.

Chorus Conducting, by Wodell; Theo. Presser & Co., Philadelphia, 1901. rev. 1930.

Control of the Breath, by Lickley and Dodds; Oxford, London, 1926.

** *Eloquent Baton, The*, by Earhart; Witmark & Sons, New York, 1931.

* *Handbook on Conducting*, by Kendrie; The H. W. Gray Co., New York, 1930.

Handbook on Conducting, by Schroeder (trans.); Augener & Co., London, 1897.

* *Interpretation of Plain Chant*, by Robertson; Oxford, London, 1937.

** *Modern Harmony*, by A. E. Hull; Augener, London (Boston Mus. Co.), 1920.

Modern Unaccompanied Song, by Bedford; Oxford, London, 1923.

Practical Points for Choral Singers, by (ed.) Vincent Mus. Co., London, 1905.

* *Pronunciation for Singers*, by Ellis; Curwen, London, 1877.

Resonance in Singing and Speaking, by Fillebrown; Ditson, Boston, 1911.

Richard Wagner on Conducting, Dannreuther; Reeves, London, 1897.

School Choirs, by Wiseman; Oxford Press, Paterson Pub., London, 1922.

* *Singing*, by Witherspoon; G. Schirmer, New York, 1925.

Song Interpretation, by Drew; Oxford Press, London, 1926.

Training of the Boys' Voices, by Johnson; Ditson, Boston, 1916.

Vocal Mastery, by Brower; Frederick A. Stokes Co., New York, 1920.

Voice, Song and Speech, by Browne; G. Putnam & Sons, New York, 1905.

Words in Singing, by Brennan; Vincent Music Co., London, 1905.

General Information and Reference

Anthems and Anthem Composers, by Foster; Novello, London, 1901.

* *Bel Canto, The*, by Klein; Oxford Press, London, 1923.

** *Biographical Dictionary of Musicians*, by Baker; G. Schirmer, New York, 1900.

Book of Common Prayer, Noted, by Merbecke; Wm. Pickering Co., London, 1844.

Church Music, by J. Curwen; Curwen, London. Studies in Worship, 1901.

Church Music, by Richardson; Longmans Green, New York, 1904.

** *Dictionary of Music*, by Grove; Macmillan, New York, also Presser, Philadelphia, 1928.

Early History of Singing, by Henderson; Longmans Green, London, 1921.

* *Early Tudor Composers*, by Flood; Oxford Press, London, 1925.

** *English Ayre, The*, by Warlock; Oxford Press, London, 1926.

English Church Composers, by Barret; Scribner & Welford, New York, 1882.

English Madrigal, The, by Fellowes; Oxford Press, London, 1925.

Evolution of the Art of Music, by Parry; Appleton, New York, 1897.

Evolution of Church Music, by Humphries; Scribner's, New York, 1896.

Geschichte des Christlichen Kirchengesanges, Hauser; Peters, Leipzig, 1834.

Great Singers on the Art of Singing, by Cooke; Presser, Philadelphia, 1921.

History of Forty Choirs, by Hastings; Mason Bros., New York, 1854.

How to Sing, by Lilli Lehmann; Macmillan, New York, 1902.

* *Hymns of the Early Church*, by Brownlie; Morgan and Scott, London, 1913.

Hymns of the Russian Church, by Brownlie; Oxford Press, London, 1920.

Introduction to the Philosophy of Education, by Demaskie-
vitch; American Book Co., 1935.

* *Life of Wm. Byrd*, by Fellowes; Oxford Press, London, 1923.

** *Madrigal Singing*, by Scott; Oxford Press, London, 1931.

Manual of Church Music, by Wm. J. (Father) Finn; Dolphin
Press, Philadelphia, 1906.

Manual of English Church Music, by Gardner; Macmillan,
New York, 1923.

Music and Musicians, by Lavignac; Holt & Co., New York,
1903.

Music in the History of the Western Church, by Ed. Dickinson;
Scribner's, New York, 1902.

Music of the Church, by La Trobe; Seeley & Burnside, London, 1831.

Musical Foundations, by Borland; Oxford Press, London, 1927.

* *New Music, The*, by Dyson; Oxford Press, London, 1924.

Organs, Organists, and Choirs, by Marshall; Curwen, London,
1886.

** *Oxford History of Music, The*, edited by Hadow; Oxford
Press, London, 1902.

* *Plainsong Accompaniment*, by Arnold; Oxford Press, London, 1927.

Psalms, The, by Richardson; Vincent Music Co., London, 1903.

Purcell, (trans. from F.) by Dupre; Oxford Press, London,
1928.

Singing of the Future, by Davies; J. Lane & Co., London, 1905.

Story of the Psalters, The, by Glass; Paul, French & Co.,
London, 1882.

* *Style of Palestrina and Dissonance, The*, by Jeppeson; Oxford, 1927.

* *Style in Music and Art*, by Parry; Macmillan, London, 1911.